To:

_____

The LORD will guide you
always.

ISAIAH 58:11

From:

_____

God's Words of Life for Women of Faith
Copyright © 2002 by Zondervan
ISBN 0-310-81360-3

All devotions taken from the: *Women of Faith Study Bible, New International Version.*® Copyright © 2001 by Zondervan. All rights reserved.

All Scripture quotations, unless otherwise noted, are taken from the *Holy Bible: New International Version®*, (North American Edition). Copyright © 1973, 1978, 1984, by International Bible Society. Used by permission of Zondervan. All rights reserved.

The "NIV" and "New International Version" trademarks are registered in the United States Patent and Trademark Office by International Bible Society.

All rights reserved. No part of this publication may be reproduced, stored in a retrieval system, or transmitted in any form or by any means—electronic, mechanical, photocopy, recording, or any other—except for brief quotations in printed reviews, without the prior permission of the publisher.

Requests for information should be addressed to:
Inspirio, The gift group of Zondervan
Grand Rapids, Michigan 49530
http://www.inspiriogifts.com

Compiler: Molly C. Detweiler
Project Manager: Janice Jacobson
Production Management: Matt Nolan
Design Manager: Amy J. Wenger
Design: Amy Peterman/Peterman Design

Printed in China

06 07 08 / 3 2 1

God's Words of Life
FOR
WOMEN
of FAITH

FROM THE
NEW INTERNATIONAL VERSION

inspirio™

God's Word of Life on

God's Words of Life on

BELIEF

You ... were included in Christ when you heard the word of truth, the gospel of your salvation. Having believed, you were marked in him with a seal, the promised Holy Spirit, who is a deposit guaranteeing our inheritance until the redemption of those who are God's possession—to the praise of his glory.

EPHESIANS 1:13-14

We believe that Jesus died and rose again and so we believe that God will bring with Jesus those who have fallen asleep in him. ... For the Lord himself will come down from heaven, with a loud command, with the voice of the archangel and with the trumpet call of God, and the dead in Christ will rise first. After that, we who are still alive and are left will be caught up together with them in the clouds to meet the Lord in the air. And so we will be with the Lord forever.

1 THESSALONIANS 4:14, 16-17

God's Words of Life on

BELIEF

Jesus said, *"If you believe, you will receive whatever you ask for in prayer."*

MATTHEW 21:22

From the beginning God chose you to be saved through the sanctifying work of the Spirit and through belief in the truth.

2 THESSALONIANS 2:13

I pray ... that the eyes of your heart may be enlightened in order that you may know the hope to which God has called you, the riches of his glorious inheritance in the saints, and his incomparably great power for us who believe. That power is like the working of his mighty strength, which he exerted in Christ when he raised him from the dead and seated him at his right hand in the heavenly realms, far above all rule and authority, power and dominion, and every title that can be given, not only in the present age but also in the one to come.

EPHESIANS 1:18-21

God's Words of Life on

BELIEF

Through Jesus you believe in God, who raised him from the dead and glorified him, and so your faith and hope are in God.

1 PETER 1:21

If you confess with your mouth, "Jesus is Lord," and believe in your heart that God raised him from the dead, you will be saved. For it is with your heart that you believe and are justified, and it is with your mouth that you confess and are saved.

ROMANS 10:9-10

Righteousness from God comes through faith in Jesus Christ to all who believe.

ROMANS 3:22

I am not ashamed of the gospel, because it is the power of God for the salvation of everyone who believes.

ROMANS 1:16

CAN YOU BELIEVE THE UNBELIEVABLE?

"I believe God can do the unbelievable." That's quite a statement! What is unbelievable to your finite, human mind becomes believable when faith steps in. Do you believe God can do even what others say is impossible? Do you believe God can give you faith to believe what seems unbelievable?

In the gospel of Mark, a desperate father comes to Jesus for healing for his little boy. The boy's father has obviously heard of Jesus, his disciples, and the many people they have healed. And even though he hopes that his son can be healed, he struggles with the unbelievable. In Mark 9:22 the father says to Jesus, "If you can do anything, take pity on us and help us".

How often do you come to God with more hope than faith? When have you hoped God would heal or help you while you still harbored doubt?

Print the words hope and faith on a piece of paper and hang it where you can see it every day. Seek Jesus' help to overcome your unbelief. He will respond as lovingly to you as he did to the father in Mark 9:23.

God's Words of Life on
COMFORT

Praise be to the God and Father of our Lord Jesus Christ, the Father of compassion and the God of all comfort, who comforts us in all our troubles, so that we can comfort those in any trouble with the comfort we ourselves have received from God.

2 CORINTHIANS 1:3-4

"As a mother comforts her child,
    so will I comfort you," says the LORD.

ISAIAH 66:13

The ransomed of the LORD will return.
    They will enter Zion with singing;
    everlasting joy will crown their heads.
Gladness and joy will overtake them,
    and sorrow and sighing will flee away.
"I, even I, am he who comforts you," says the LORD.

ISAIAH 51:11-12

God's Words of Life on

COMFORT

The Spirit of the Sovereign LORD is on me,
   because the LORD has anointed me
   to preach good news to the poor.
He has sent me to bind up the brokenhearted,
   to proclaim freedom for the captives
   and release from darkness for the prisoners,
to proclaim the year of the LORD's favor
   and the day of vengeance of our God,
to comfort all who mourn,
   and provide for those who grieve in Zion—
to bestow on them a crown of beauty
   instead of ashes,
the oil of gladness
   instead of mourning,
and a garment of praise
   instead of a spirit of despair.

ISAIAH 61:1-3

May your unfailing love be my comfort, O LORD,
   according to your promise to your servant.

PSALM 119:76

11

God's Words of Life on

COMFORT

Shout for joy, O heavens;
    rejoice, O earth;
    burst into song, O mountains!
For the LORD comforts his people
    and will have compassion on his afflicted ones.

ISAIAH 49:13

The LORD your God is with you,
    he is mighty to save.
He will take great delight in you,
    he will quiet you with his love,
    he will rejoice over you with singing.

ZEPHANIAH 3:17

This I call to mind
    and therefore I have hope:
Because of the LORD'S great love we are not consumed,
    for his compassions never fail.
They are new every morning;
    great is your faithfulness.

LAMENTATIONS 3:21-23

God's Words of Life on

COMFORT

Surely God is my salvation;
   I will trust and not be afraid.
The LORD, the LORD, is my strength and my song;
   he has become my salvation.

ISAIAH 12:2

How priceless is your unfailing love, O LORD!
Both high and low among men
   find refuge in the shadow of your wings.

PSALM 36:7

You will increase my honor
   and comfort me once again, O LORD.

PSALM 71:21

God's Words of Life on

COMFORT

The LORD is my shepherd, I shall not be in want.
　　He makes me lie down in green pastures,
he leads me beside quiet waters,
　　he restores my soul.
He guides me in paths of righteousness
　　for his name's sake.
Even though I walk
　　through the valley of the shadow of death,
I will fear no evil,
　　for you are with me;
your rod and your staff,
　　they comfort me.
You prepare a table before me
　　in the presence of my enemies.
You anoint my head with oil;
　　my cup overflows.
Surely goodness and love will follow me
　　all the days of my life,
and I will dwell in the house of the LORD
　　forever.

PSALM 23

GOD LONGS TO COMFORT YOU

Does God ever seem too far away, too fearsome, too holy? How can this kind of God be a comfort to you? You know in your mind that God can be trusted, yet your heart resists. Jesus knows your fears and doubts. He came to this earth to show you the Father (John 14:9-10 and Hebrews 1:3). He came so you could know him and know the Father's heart—a heart of love, gentleness, and compassion (Psalm 103:8). When you know Jesus, you also know the Father (John 14:7).

Are you walking a difficult path right now? God is longing to comfort you. He has a plan for you that includes building you up so that you may help others in their times of need.

Find a quiet place where you will not be interrupted and speak with Jesus. Allow this to be a time of slow, thoughtful meditation. You may want to picture taking the pain in your heart and actually handing it to Jesus. His arms are always open, ready to take your pain and offer you comfort.

God's Words of Life on

COURAGE

Be strong and courageous. Do not be terrified; do not be discouraged, for the LORD your God will be with you wherever you go.

JOSHUA 1:9

There is no fear in love. But perfect love drives out fear.

1 JOHN 4:18

God has said,
"Never will I leave you;
*   never will I forsake you."*
So we say with confidence,
"The Lord is my helper; I will not be afraid.
*   What can man do to me?"*

HEBREWS 13:5-6

Jesus said, "Do not be afraid, little flock, for your Father has been pleased to give you the kingdom."

LUKE 12:32

God's Words of Life on

COURAGE

Jesus said, *"Peace I leave with you; my peace I give you. I do not give to you as the world gives. Do not let your hearts be troubled and do not be afraid."*

JOHN 14:27

When I am afraid,
I will trust in you.
In God, whose word I praise,
in God I trust; I will not be afraid.

PSALM 56:3-4

You came near when I called you,
and you said, "Do not fear."
O LORD, you took up my case;
you redeemed my life.

LAMENTATIONS 3:57-58

God's Words of Life on

COURAGE

Blessed is the man who trusts in the LORD,
whose confidence is in him.
He will be like a tree planted by the water
that sends out its roots by the stream.
It does not fear when heat comes;
its leaves are always green.
It has no worries in a year of drought
and never fails to bear fruit.

JEREMIAH 17:7-8

This is what the LORD says ...
"Fear not, for I have redeemed you;
I have summoned you by name; you are mine.
When you pass through the waters,
I will be with you;
and when you pass through the rivers,
they will not sweep over you.
When you walk through the fire,
you will not be burned;
the flames will not set you ablaze."

ISAIAH 43:1-2

FACING GOLIATH

In 1 Samuel 17 we find the familiar story of David and Goliath. A giant Philistine warrior is taunting the Israelites and their king, Saul. They are cowering in fear, seeing Goliath's threats not only as a physical danger, but also an attack on their personal reputations and the reputation of their nation.

Then along comes a very young shepherd boy named David who sees more in the giant's words. He hears them as an affront to God. Goliath certainly intimidates David, but David isn't trusting his own abilities. His is trusting the power of Almighty God.

When you trust God rather than yourself, you can depend on his help. Your courage in difficult circumstances may be misunderstood by others, as was David's. People may try to dissuade you from trusting God. But if you make it clear that your courage comes from your confidence in God's abilities, not your own, then God will receive the glory for the outcome.

Fear is a normal human reaction to frightening and overwhelming circumstances. Fear is an opportunity to expand your faith in God. Bring your fears, anxieties, and concerns to God, the only One who is fully able to defeat your Goliaths.

EMOTIONS

Is anyone happy? Let him sing songs of praise.

JAMES 5:13

In my anguish I cried to the LORD,
    and he answered by setting me free.

PSALM 118:5

A happy heart makes the face cheerful.

PROVERBS 15:13

As the deer pants for streams of water,
    so my soul pants for you, O God.
My soul thirsts for God, for the living God.

PSALM 42:1-2

May the righteous be glad and rejoice before God;
    may they be happy and joyful.

PSALM 68:3

God's Words of Life on

EMOTIONS

Why are you downcast, O my soul?
    Why so disturbed within me?
Put your hope in God,
    for I will yet praise him,
    my Savior and my God.

PSALM 42:5-6

Though you have made me see troubles, many and
bitter,
    you will restore my life again;
from the depths of the earth
    you will again bring me up.
You will increase my honor
    and comfort me once again.

PSALM 71:20-20

Blessed are those who mourn,
    for they will be comforted.

MATTHEW 5:4

God's Words of Life on

EMOTIONS

Turn to me and be gracious to me, LORD,
    for I am lonely and afflicted.
The troubles of my heart have multiplied;
    free me from my anguish.
Look upon my affliction and my distress
    and take away all my sins. ...
Guard my life and rescue me;
    let me not be put to shame,
    for I take refuge in you.
May integrity and uprightness protect me,
    because my hope is in you.

PSALM 25:16-18, 20-21

You turned my wailing into dancing;
    you removed my sackcloth and clothed me
with joy,
that my heart may sing to you and not be silent,
    O LORD my God, I will give you thanks forever.

PSALM 30:11

CHOOSING TO BE HAPPY

The adage "Happiness is a choice" could be applied to Proverbs 17:22: "A cheerful heart is good medicine." When circumstances threaten to crush people's spirits and sink them in gloom, they need the powerful "medicine" of joy more than ever. Solomon is probably not advocating a superficial "grin and bear it" or "put on a happy face" mentality, but instead, a deep, abiding faith that all will be well for those who trust God.

Life's trials and disappointments can indeed feel crushing at times, be we need not roll over in despair. Rather, the prescription for happiness is at our fingertips. We can cultivate our faith in the profoundly good news of the One who encourages us with these words: "I have told you these things, so that in me you may have peace. In this world you will have trouble. But take heart! I have overcome the world" (John 16:33).

God's Words of Life on

ENCOURAGEMENT

May our Lord Jesus Christ himself and God our Father, who loved us and by his grace gave us eternal encouragement and good hope, encourage your hearts and strengthen you in every good deed and word.

2 THESSALONIANS 2:16-17

Paul said, "I have great confidence in you; I take great pride in you. I am greatly encouraged; in all our troubles my joy knows no bounds."

2 CORINTHIANS 7:4

I was overcome by trouble and sorrow.
Then I called on the name of the LORD:
"O LORD, save me!"
The LORD is gracious and righteous;
our God is full of compassion.
The LORD protects the simplehearted;
when I was in great need, he saved me.

PSALM 116:3-6

God's Words of Life on

ENCOURAGEMENT

Everything that was written in the past was written to teach us, so that through endurance and the encouragement of the Scriptures we might have hope.

ROMANS 15:4

*The LORD upholds all those who fall
   and lifts up all who are bowed down.*

PSALM 145:14

*Blessed is he whose help is the God of Jacob,
   whose hope is in the LORD his God,
the Maker of heaven and earth,
   the sea, and everything in them—
   the LORD, who remains faithful forever.
He upholds the cause of the oppressed
   and gives food to the hungry.
The LORD sets prisoners free,
   the LORD gives sight to the blind,
the LORD lifts up those who are bowed down,
   the LORD loves the righteous.*

PSALM 146:5-8

ENCOURAGEMENT

I lift up my eyes to the hills—
     where does my help come from?
My help comes from the LORD,
     the Maker of heaven and earth.

PSALM 121:1-2

As God's fellow workers we urge you not to receive
God's grace in vain. For he says,
     "In the time of my favor I heard you,
     and in the day of salvation I helped you."
I tell you, now is the time of God's favor, now is the
day of salvation

2 CORINTHIANS 6:1-2

The LORD himself goes before you and will be with
you; he will never leave you nor forsake you. Do not
be afraid; do not be discouraged.

DEUTERONOMY 31:8

You hear, O LORD, the desire of the afflicted;
     you encourage them, and you listen to their cry.

PSALM 10:17

YOU CAN OVERCOME

Life is hard, and most people get through it simply by coping. If people are unhappy in marriage, parenthood, career, or friendships, they mostly do the best they can. They cope. But is this the way God wants believers to live?

Jesus said, "Take heart! I have overcome the world" (John 16:33). You are an overcomer too because of Jesus Christ. "Who is it that overcomes the world? Only he who believes that Jesus is the Son of God" (1 John 5:5).

When trials, troubles, persecutions, disasters, or attacks come, don't give in to fear and discouragement. God will supply the strength you need to overcome in your adversity. He will help you feel encouraged again, even in the midst of your struggles.

Think about some of the things in which you're experiencing difficulty right now. Are you merely coping in these areas instead of overcoming? Express your thanks to God in prayer for his love and the power he makes available to you so that you can do more than cope—you can overcome. If you feel weak, ask him for his strength. He is able to supply all your needs (Philippians 4:19).

God's Words of Life on

FAITH

Everyone born of God overcomes the world. This is the victory that has overcome the world, even our faith.

1 JOHN 5:4

Now for a little while you may have had to suffer grief in all kinds of trials. These have come so that your faith—of greater worth than gold, which perishes even though refined by fire—may be proved genuine and may result in praise, glory and honor when Jesus Christ is revealed.

1 PETER 1:6-7

The LORD rewards every man for his righteousness and faithfulness.

1 SAMUEL 26:23

To the faithful you show yourself faithful, O LORD, to the blameless you show yourself blameless.

2 SAMUEL 22:26

God's Words of Life on
FAITH

Though you have not seen Jesus, you love him; and even though you do not see him now, you believe in him and are filled with an inexpressible and glorious joy, for you are receiving the goal of your faith, the salvation of your souls.

1 PETER 1:8-9

Since we have been justified through faith, we have peace with God through our Lord Jesus Christ, through whom we have gained access by faith into this grace in which we now stand.

ROMANS 5:1-2

Faithfulness springs forth from the earth,
and righteousness looks down from heaven.
The LORD will indeed give what is good,
and our land will yield its harvest.

PSALM 85:11-12

God's Words of Life on

FAITH

Praise be to the God and Father of our Lord Jesus Christ! In his great mercy he has given us new birth into a living hope through the resurrection of Jesus Christ from the dead, and into an inheritance that can never perish, spoil or fade—kept in heaven for you, who through faith are shielded by God's power until the coming of the salvation that is ready to be revealed in the last time.

1 PETER 1:3-5

I will sing of the LORD's great love forever;
    with my mouth I will make your faithfulness
    known through all generations.
I will declare that your love stands firm forever,
    that you established your faithfulness
    in heaven itself.

PSALM 89:1-2

Let us hold unswervingly to the hope we profess, for God who promised is faithful.

HEBREWS 10:23

God's Words of Life on

FAITH

Let us fix our eyes on Jesus, the author and perfecter of our faith, who for the joy set before him endured the cross, scorning its shame, and sat down at the right hand of the throne of God. Consider him who endured such opposition from sinful men, so that you will not grow weary and lose heart.

HEBREWS 12:2-3

Faith is being sure of what we hope for and certain of what we do not see.

HEBREWS 11:1

By faith Moses, when he had grown up, refused to be known as the son of Pharaoh's daughter. He chose to be mistreated along with the people of God rather than to enjoy the pleasures of sin for a short time. He regarded disgrace for the sake of Christ as of greater value than the treasures of Egypt, because he was looking ahead to his reward.

HEBREWS 11:24-26

FAITH

I have fought the good fight, I have finished the race, I have kept the faith. Now there is in store for me the crown of righteousness, which the Lord, the righteous Judge, will award to me on that day—and not only to me, but also to all who have longed for his appearing.

2 TIMOTHY 4:7-8

The Lord is faithful, and he will strengthen and protect you from the evil one.

2 THESSALONIANS 3:3

In Christ and through faith in him we may approach God with freedom and confidence.

EPHESIANS 3:12

Jesus said, "I tell you the truth, if you have faith as small as a mustard seed, you can say to this mountain, 'Move from here to there' and it will move. Nothing will be impossible for you."

MATTHEW 17:20

THE GIFT OF FAITH

Faith is a gift of God just as salvation is a gift of grace. It cannot be earned or conjured up. You won't have faith by saying, "I have faith; I have faith." Faith is a sovereign gift from God as he reveals Christ to us in his word.

True faith is experienced—not just affirmed. It is your heart's "Aha!" when you discover the hope and power found only in a relationship with Jesus Christ. That faith drives all you do. That faith compels you to do God's will.

If you have not accepted the gift of faith that the Holy Spirit offers, receive his grace and allow him to bring a new revelation to your heart of who Jesus is. If you have embraced the truth of Jesus; if, by faith, you know him in a way you cannot prove but will never deny, you can stand with the hosts of heaven and shout, "Worthy is the Lamb!" (Revelation 5:12) Spend some time in prayer simply praising God—in your own unique way—for the gifts of grace, faith and, most of all, Jesus.

God's Words of Life on

FAMILY

I have no greater joy than to hear that my children are walking in the truth.

3 JOHN 1:4

Both the one who makes men holy and those who are made holy are of the same family. So Jesus is not ashamed to call them brothers.

HEBREWS 2:11

Children, obey your parents in the Lord, for this is right. "Honor your father and mother"—which is the first commandment with a promise—"that it may go well with you and that you may enjoy long life on the earth."

EPHESIANS 6:1-3

As we have opportunity, let us do good to all people, especially to those who belong to the family of believers.

GALATIANS 6:10

God's Words of Life on

FAMILY

The Spirit himself testifies with our spirit that we are God's children. Now if we are children, then we are heirs—heirs of God and co-heirs with Christ, if indeed we share in his sufferings in order that we may also share in his glory.

ROMANS 8:16-17

To all who received Christ, to those who believed in his name, he gave the right to become children of God—children born not of natural descent ... but born of God.

JOHN 1:12-13

As a father has compassion on his children,
        so the LORD has compassion
        on those who fear him.

PSALM 103:13

Children's children are a crown to the aged,
        and parents are the pride of their children.

PROVERBS 17:6

God's Words of Life on

FAMILY

From everlasting to everlasting
	the LORD's love is with those who fear him,
and his righteousness with their children's children—
	with those who keep his covenant
and remember to obey his precepts.

PSALM 103:17-18

For every house is built by someone, but God is the builder of everything. Moses was faithful as a servant in all God's house, testifying to what would be said in the future. But Christ is faithful as a son over God's house. And we are his house, if we hold on to our courage and the hope of which we boast.

HEBREWS 3:4-6

Dear friends, let us love one another, for love comes from God. Everyone who loves has been born of God and knows God.

1 JOHN 4:7

THE FAMILY OF GOD

Dependent. Connected. Related. These are just a few of the words that describe the community life of first-century Christians. In our individualistic culture, the intimacy of the early followers of Christ might surprise us a little and even put us off. These first-century Christians voluntarily shared their resources and willingly invested their hard-earned money in the lives of others. They met in the temple regularly to feed on the heavenly bread of the Word of God. They gathered in their homes to break bread and enjoyed fellowship with each other. Their lives were intertwined and interconnected.

God has blessed you with not only the family you were born into, but also his family, where God is the father and your fellow Christians are your brothers and sisters. You can share each other's joys and sorrows and you always feel that you belong. What a wonderful gift from God!

God's Words of Life on

FORGIVENESS

If we confess our sins, God is faithful and just and will forgive us our sins and purify us from all unrighteousness.

1 JOHN 1:9

When we were overwhelmed by sins,
        you forgave our transgressions, O LORD.

PSALM 65:3

God has rescued us from the dominion of darkness and brought us into the kingdom of the Son he loves, in whom we have redemption, the forgiveness of sins.

COLOSSIANS 1:13-14

If you, O LORD, kept a record of sins,
        O LORD, who could stand?
But with you there is forgiveness;
        therefore you are feared.
I wait for the LORD, my soul waits,
        and in his word I put my hope.

PSALM 130:3-5

God's Words of Life on
FORGIVENESS

Let us draw near to God with a sincere heart in full assurance of faith, having our hearts sprinkled to cleanse us from a guilty conscience and having our bodies washed with pure water.

HEBREWS 10:22

You are forgiving and good, O LORD, abounding in love to all who call to you.

PSALM 86:5

Everyone who believes in Jesus receives forgiveness of sins through his name.

ACTS 10:43

Praise the LORD, O my soul, and forget not all his benefits— who forgives all your sins and heals all your diseases.

PSALM 103:2-3

FORGIVENESS

I acknowledged my sin to you
and did not cover up my iniquity.
I said, "I will confess
my transgressions to the LORD"—
and you forgave
the guilt of my sin.
Therefore let everyone who is godly pray to you
while you may be found;
surely when the mighty waters rise,
they will not reach him.
You are my hiding place;
you will protect me from trouble
and surround me with songs of deliverance.

PSALM 32:5-7

In Jesus we have redemption through his blood, the
forgiveness of sins, in accordance with the riches of
God's grace that he lavished on us with all wisdom
and understanding.

EPHESIANS 1:7-8

FORGIVENESS

As high as the heavens are above the earth,
    so great is God's love for those who fear him;
as far as the east is from the west,
    so far has he removed our transgressions from us.
As a father has compassion on his children,
    so the LORD has compassion
    on those who fear him.

PSALM 103:11-13

"I will sprinkle clean water on you, and you will be
clean; I will cleanse you from all your impurities. ... I
will give you a new heart and put a new spirit in
you; I will remove from you your heart of stone and
give you a heart of flesh," says the LORD.

EZEKIEL 36:25-26

Blessed is he
    whose transgressions are forgiven,
    whose sins are covered.
Blessed is the man
    whose sin the LORD does not count against him.

PSALM 32:1-2

God's Words of Life on

FORGIVENESS

Cleanse me with hyssop, and I will be clean, O Lord;
wash me, and I will be whiter than snow.

PSALM 51:7

"Come now, let us reason together,"
says the LORD.
"Though your sins are like scarlet,
they shall be as white as snow;
though they are red as crimson,
they shall be like wool."

ISAIAH 1:18

Have mercy on me, O God,
according to your unfailing love;
according to your great compassion
blot out my transgressions.
Wash away all my iniquity
and cleanse me from my sin.

PSALM 51:1-2

THE GIFT OF FORGIVENESS

Did you know that you have a crown? God has crowned you with love and compassion (Psalm 103:4). Your crown hasn't been given to you as a reward but as a mark and as a symbol of your royalty. You have God's mark, the Holy Spirit (Ephesians 1:13), and you are God's child (1 John 3:1)—that makes you royalty. Your Father wants to help you when you are in need and to forgive you when you sin.

Forgiveness, whether human or divine, is an indescribable gift. Sometimes it's hard to accept forgiveness from God. You simply can't forgive yourself—even when God already has. Remember that God "does not treat [you] as [your] sins deserve" (Psalm 103:10). When you confess your sin, it's gone (Psalm 103:12). If you have not asked for forgiveness, why not do so now? If you have already sought forgiveness but you lack assurance, ask for God's grace to be able to accept what he has already given you—the gift of forgiveness.

God's Words of Life on

FRIENDSHIP

A friend loves at all times.

PROVERBS 17:17

Perfume and incense bring joy to the heart,
*   and the pleasantness of one's friend springs*
from his earnest counsel.

PROVERBS 27:9

Jesus said, "Greater love has no one than this, that
he lay down his life for his friends. You are my
friends if you do what I command. I no longer call
you servants, because a servant does not know his
master's business. Instead, I have called you friends,
for everything that I learned from my Father I have
made known to you."

JOHN 15:13-15

Love one another deeply, from the heart.

1 PETER 1:22

God's Words of Life on FRIENDSHIP

Two are better than one,
because they have a good return for their work:
If one falls down,
his friend can help him up.
But pity the man who falls
and has no one to help him up!
Also, if two lie down together, they will keep warm.
But how can one keep warm alone?
Though one may be overpowered,
two can defend themselves.
A cord of three strands is not quickly broken.

ECCLESIASTES 4:9-12

As God's chosen people, holy and dearly loved, clothe yourselves with compassion, kindness, humility, gentleness and patience. Bear with each other and forgive whatever grievances you may have against one another. Forgive as the Lord forgave you. And over all these virtues put on love, which binds them all together in perfect unity.

COLOSSIANS 3:12-14

FRIENDSHIP

A kindhearted woman gains respect.

PROVERBS 11:16

A generous man will prosper;
*   he who refreshes others will himself be*
refreshed.

PROVERBS 11:25

An anxious heart weighs a man down,
*   but a kind word cheers him up.*

PROVERBS 12:25

He who covers over an offense promotes love,
*   but whoever repeats the matter separates*
*   close friends.*

PROVERBS 17:9

He who walks with the wise grows wise.

PROVERBS 13:20

INTIMACY WITH GOD

Does the idea of intimacy with God frighten you? *"Who could be intimate with a holy, righteous God?"* you ask. Yes, God is holy and righteous, and he is also loving and compassionate. God reveals himself in Scripture as a father and as a husband. He provides for you and protects you as a loving father. As your husband he desires to meet your need for intimacy.

God is in pursuit of you. He wants an intimate relationship with you—one that will last forever, one that will satisfy your deepest needs. You can respond to God by allowing him to draw you into his loving arms. Your life, your relationships, your reactions—all will be affected by God's embrace.

Just like a very best friend, God longs to listen to you and talk to you in turn. Take time this very day to nurture the best friendship of them all: your friendship with God.

God's Words of Life on

FUTURE

"*I know the plans I have for you,*" *declares the*
LORD, "*plans to prosper you and not to harm you,*
plans to give you hope and a future."

JEREMIAH 29:11

Consider the blameless, observe the upright;
     there is a future for the man of peace.

PSALM 37:37

Know also that wisdom is sweet to your soul;
     if you find it, there is a future hope for you,
     and your hope will not be cut off.

PROVERBS 24:14

Many, O LORD *my God,*
     are the wonders you have done.
The things you planned for us
     no one can recount to you;
were I to speak and tell of them,
     they would be too many to declare.

PSALM 40:5

FUTURE

Delight yourself in the LORD
and he will give you the desires of your heart.
Commit your way to the LORD;
trust in him and he will do this:
He will make your righteousness shine like the dawn,
the justice of your cause like the noonday sun.

PSALM 37:4-6

No eye has seen,
no ear has heard,
no mind has conceived
what God has prepared for those who love him.

1 CORINTHIANS 2:9

"Store up for yourselves treasures in heaven, where moth and rust do not destroy, and where thieves do not break in and steal. For where your treasure is, there your heart will be also."

MATTHEW 6:20-21

God's Words of Life on

FUTURE

My frame was not hidden from you, LORD,
  when I was made in the secret place.
When I was woven together in the depths of the earth,
  your eyes saw my unformed body.
All the days ordained for me
  were written in your book
  before one of them came to be.

PSALM 139:15-16

Forgetting what is behind and straining toward
what is ahead, I press on toward the goal to win the
prize for which God has called me heavenward in
Christ Jesus.

PHILIPPIANS 3:13-14

Surely goodness and love will follow me
  all the days of my life,
and I will dwell in the house of the LORD
  forever.

PSALM 23:6

Devotional Thought on Future
HOPE AND A FUTURE

In a world full of uncertainty, it's hard to know how to feel about the future. While we all hope for brighter days ahead, many times the present seems to speak of only impending darkness. When the world around us causes us to lose hope, that's when we must look to the words of the One who knows the future and has it in his hands.

The dazzling words of Jeremiah 29:11-13 were not only words of comfort and confidence from the prophet to the captive Israelites, they are also God's message for us today: "I know the plans I have for you," declares the LORD, "plans to prosper you and not to harm you, plans to give you hope and a future. Then you will call upon me and come and pray to me, and I will listen to you. You will seek me and find me when you seek me with all your heart."

God knows the future and wants us to trust him for the journey ahead. No matter how bleak the circumstances, God promises "hope and a future."

GOD'S PRESENCE

I am convinced that neither death nor life, neither angels nor demons, neither the present nor the future, nor any powers, neither height nor depth, nor anything else in all creation, will be able to separate us from the love of God that is in Christ Jesus our Lord.

ROMANS 8:38-39

Come near to God and he will come near to you.

JAMES 4:8

No one has ever seen God; but if we love one another, God lives in us and his love is made complete in us.

1 JOHN 4:12

God has said,
"Never will I leave you;
*   never will I forsake you."*

HEBREWS 13:5

God's Words of Life on

GOD'S PRESENCE

Where can I go from your Spirit?
  Where can I flee from your presence?
If I go up to the heavens, you are there, O LORD;
  if I make my bed in the depths, you are there.
If I rise on the wings of the dawn,
  if I settle on the far side of the sea,
even there your hand will guide me,
  your right hand will hold me fast.

PSALM 139:7-10

You have made known to me the path of life, O LORD;
  you will fill me with joy in your presence,
  with eternal pleasures at your right hand.

PSALM 16:11

In my integrity you uphold me
  and set me in your presence forever.
Praise be to the LORD, the God of Israel,
  from everlasting to everlasting.

PSALM 41:12-13

God's Words of Life on

GOD'S PRESENCE

Jesus said, "I will ask the Father, and he will give you another Counselor to be with you forever—the Spirit of truth. The world cannot accept him, because it neither sees him nor knows him. But you know him, for he lives with you and will be in you. I will not leave you as orphans; I will come to you."

JOHN 14:16-18

"Fear not, for I have redeemed you;
*   I have summoned you by name; you are mine.*
When you pass through the waters,
*   I will be with you;*
and when you pass through the rivers,
*   they will not sweep over you.*
When you walk through the fire,
*   you will not be burned;*
*   the flames will not set you ablaze," says the LORD.*

ISAIAH 43:1-2

Jesus said, "Surely I am with you always, to the very end of the age."

MATTHEW 28:20

Devotional Thought on God's Presence

THIRSTING FOR GOD

The words of Psalm 63:1-8 are the words of one who has been in God's presence, has tasted the spiritual beauty of God and has no other desire than to be in God's presence again. David, the writer of this psalm, declares, "My soul thirsts for you ... I have seen you in the sanctuary and beheld your ... glory" (Psalm 63:1-2). To behold God's glory is an awesome and life-changing event.

If you desire to enter God's presence, go to him in prayer. He is longing to come to you, to refresh you, to love you. Do as David does: remember. In a journal or a notebook, record times in the past when God seemed near; list his blessings to you; record reasons to rejoice and to praise him for who he is and for what he has done. Build up your faith by writing about who Jesus is and who you are in him. It is in Jesus that you will have confidence to approach the throne of God (Ephesians 3:12; Hebrews 10:19-23) and enjoy the sweetness of his presence.

GOD'S WILL

Jesus said, "Whoever does God's will is my brother and sister and mother."

MARK 3:35

Do not conform any longer to the pattern of this world, but be transformed by the renewing of your mind. Then you will be able to test and approve what God's will is—his good, pleasing and perfect will.

ROMANS 12:2

The world and its desires pass away, but the man who does the will of God lives forever.

1 JOHN 2:17

*Teach me to do your will,
    for you are my God,
may your good Spirit
    lead me on level ground.*

PSALM 143:10

GOD'S WILL

Do not forget to do good and to share with others, for with such sacrifices God is pleased.

HEBREWS 13:16

Jesus said, "I have come down from heaven not to do my will but to do the will of him who sent me. And this is the will of him who sent me, that I shall lose none of all that he has given me, but raise them up at the last day. For my Father's will is that every-one who looks to the Son and believes in him shall have eternal life, and I will raise him up at the last day."

JOHN 6:38-40

May the God of peace ... equip you with everything good for doing his will, and may he work in us what is pleasing to him, through Jesus Christ, to whom be glory for ever and ever.

HEBREWS 13:20-21

God's Words of Life on
GOD'S WILL

This is the confidence we have in approaching God: that if we ask anything according to his will, he hears us. And if we know that he hears us—whatever we ask—we know that we have what we asked of him.

1 JOHN 5:14-15

It is God who works in you to will and to act according to his good purpose.

PHILIPPIANS 2:13

To the man who pleases him, God gives wisdom, knowledge and happiness.

ECCLESIASTES 2:26

Be joyful always; pray continually; give thanks in all circumstances, for this is God's will for you in Christ Jesus.

1 THESSALONIANS 5:16-18

UNCHARTED WATERS

In Joshua 3:1-17 we read that Joshua stands with the people of Israel at the edge of the Jordan River. Normally only about a hundred feet wide, the river is at flood stage—much wider and treacherous to cross. How will Joshua get all the Israelites, including the women and children, across? And where will he lead them then?

God has a plan. He himself will lead them. The waters of the Jordan part, but only when the priests walk forward by faith, and their feet touch the water's edge (Joshua 3:15-16). Have you ever sensed God leading you into uncharted waters, to a place you've never been before? How can you discover God's will?

When you pray, ask God to reveal his will to you. Expect an answer, but don't be surprised if you must wait. If you are a believer in Jesus, God has sent his Holy Spirit to guide you (Psalm 73:23-24; John 16:13). You may however, have to put your feet into the water first, as the priests did at the edge of the Jordan. That means you may have to step out in faith and obey God's clear commands before you will see the path of his will opened in front of you.

God's Words of Life on

GRACE

Because of his great love for us, God, who is rich in mercy, made us alive with Christ even when we were dead in transgressions—it is by grace you have been saved.

EPHESIANS 2:4-5

All have sinned and fall short of the glory of God, and are justified freely by his grace through the redemption that came by Christ Jesus.

ROMANS 3:23-24

The LORD longs to be gracious to you;
*   he rises to show you compassion.*
For the LORD is a God of justice.
*   Blessed are all who wait for him!*

ISAIAH 30:18

It is by grace you have been saved, through faith—and this not from yourselves, it is the gift of God—not by works, so that no one can boast.

EPHESIANS 2:8-9

God's Words of Life on

GRACE

You know the grace of our Lord Jesus Christ, that though he was rich, yet for your sakes he became poor, so that you through his poverty might become rich.

2 CORINTHIANS 8:9

God demonstrates his own love for us in this: While we were still sinners, Christ died for us.

ROMANS 5:8

The Word became flesh and made his dwelling among us. We have seen his glory, the glory of the One and Only, who came from the Father, full of grace and truth. ... From the fullness of his grace we have all received one blessing after another For the law was given through Moses; grace and truth came through Jesus Christ.

JOHN 1:14, 16-17

The LORD your God is gracious and compassionate. He will not turn his face from you if you return to him.

2 CHRONICLES 30:9

GRACE

God is able to make all grace abound to you, so that in all things at all times, having all that you need, you will abound in every good work.

2 CORINTHIANS 9:8

The LORD is compassionate and gracious,
*   slow to anger, abounding in love.*
He will not always accuse,
*   nor will he harbor his anger forever;*
he does not treat us as our sins deserve
*   or repay us according to our iniquities.*
For as high as the heavens are above the earth,
*   so great is his love for those who fear him;*
as far as the east is from the west,
*   so far has he removed our transgressions from us.*
As a father has compassion on his children,
*   so the LORD has compassion*
*   on those who fear him;*
for he knows how we are formed,
*   he remembers that we are dust.*

PSALM 103:8-14

God's Words of Life on

GRACE

When the kindness and love of God our Savior
appeared, he saved us, not because of righteous
things we had done, but because of his mercy. He
saved us through the washing of rebirth and renewal
by the Holy Spirit, whom he poured out on us
generously through Jesus Christ our Savior, so that,
having been justified by his grace, we might become
heirs having the hope of eternal life.

TITUS 3:4-7

Grace, mercy and peace from God the Father and
from Jesus Christ, the Father's Son, will be with us in
truth and love.

2 JOHN 1:3

We do not have a high priest who is unable to sym-
pathize with our weaknesses, but we have one who
has been tempted in every way, just as we are— yet
was without sin. Let us then approach the throne of
grace with confidence, so that we may receive mercy
and find grace to help us in our time of need.

HEBREWS 4:15-16

God's Words of Life on

GRACE

Grace and peace be yours in abundance through the knowledge of God and of Jesus our Lord. His divine power has given us everything we need for life and godliness through our knowledge of him who called us by his own glory and goodness.

2 PETER 1:2-3

To each one of us grace has been given as Christ apportioned it.

EPHESIANS 4:7

God chose us in Christ before the creation of the world to be holy and blameless in his sight. In love he predestined us to be adopted as his sons through Jesus Christ, in accordance with his pleasure and will—to the praise of his glorious grace, which he has freely given us in the One he loves. In him we have redemption through his blood, the forgiveness of sins, in accordance with the riches of God's grace that he lavished on us with all wisdom and under-standing.

EPHESIANS 1:4-8

GETTING WHAT YOU DON'T DESERVE

Grace is unmerited favor and assistance. If you receive a gift or a favor without earning it or deserving it, you are receiving grace. In Ephesians 1:3-10 you can read of the incredible blessings God has poured out on you by his grace. He has chosen you, adopted you as his child, redeemed you, forgiven you and made known to you the mystery of his will—righteousness by grace through Christ. All this was done to reveal "his glorious grace" (Ephesians 1:6).

In thanks, offer yourself and your praises to God. Allow the Holy Spirit to transform you so that you will reflect God's glory as you become more and more like Jesus. What blessings you have in Jesus and what freedom you have in knowing that your salvation—as well as your entire Christian life—is based on God's grace, not your own efforts (2 Timothy 1:8-9)!

God's Words of Life on

GROWTH

Like newborn babies, crave pure spiritual milk, so that by it you may grow up in your salvation, now that you have tasted that the Lord is good.

1 PETER 2:2-3

Speaking the truth in love, we will in all things grow up into him who is the Head, that is, Christ. From him the whole body, joined and held together by every supporting ligament, grows and builds itself up in love, as each part does its work.

EPHESIANS 4:15-16

The righteous will flourish like a palm tree,
    they will grow like a cedar of Lebanon;
planted in the house of the LORD,
    they will flourish in the courts of our God.
They will still bear fruit in old age,
    they will stay fresh and green,
proclaiming, "The LORD is upright;
    he is my Rock, and there is no wickedness in him."

PSALM 92:12-15

GROWTH

Your hands made me and formed me, LORD;
give me understanding to learn your commands.

PSALM 119:73

Instruct a wise man and he will be wiser still;
teach a righteous man
and he will add to his learning.
"The fear of the LORD is the beginning of wisdom,
and knowledge of the Holy One is
understanding."

PROVERBS 9:9-10

All Scripture is God-breathed and is useful for
teaching, rebuking, correcting and training in
righteousness, so that the man of God may be
thoroughly equipped for every good work.

2 TIMOTHY 3:16-17

God's Words of Life on

GROWTH

Anyone who lives on milk, being still an infant, is not acquainted with the teaching about righteousness. But solid food is for the mature, who by constant use have trained themselves to distinguish good from evil. Therefore let us leave the elementary teachings about Christ and go on to maturity.

HEBREWS 5:13-6:1

If any of you lacks wisdom, he should ask God, who gives generously to all without finding fault, and it will be given to him.

JAMES 1:5

It was God who gave some to be apostles, some to be prophets, some to be evangelists, and some to be pastors and teachers, to prepare God's people for works of service, so that the body of Christ may be built up until we all reach unity in the faith and in the knowledge of the Son of God and become mature, attaining to the whole measure of the fullness of Christ.

EPHESIANS 4:11-13

YOU *CAN* PLEASE GOD

Many believers find it hard to imagine that they can actually please God. They have the notion that God is keeping score of their faults, writing down every sin and mistake. The Scripture makes it quite clear that God is thrilled with you at times (Zephaniah 3:17). According to Colossians 1:10-12, there are four things that please God: Bearing fruit in good works, growing in the knowledge of God, having great endurance and patience, and joyfully giving thanks to the Father.

Second Peter 1:5-8 gives us a challenge and an encouragement: "Make every effort to add to your faith goodness; and to goodness, knowledge; and to knowledge, self-control; and to self-control, perseverance; and to perseverance, godliness; and to godliness, brotherly kindness; and to brotherly kindness, love."

Because God has given you everything you need, by sending his Holy Spirit to dwell in you and by infusing you with his power, you can please him by living a godly life. The more time you spend with a person, the more you become like that person. So it is when we spend time with Jesus. Remember: true Christianity is not a religion but a relationship.

GUIDANCE

The LORD will guide you always;
   he will satisfy your needs in a sun-scorched land
   and will strengthen your frame.
You will be like a well-watered garden,
   like a spring whose waters never fail.

ISAIAH 58:11

God is our God for ever and ever;
   he will be our guide even to the end.

PSALM 48:14

"When he, the Spirit of truth, comes, he will guide
you into all truth. He will not speak on his own; he
will speak only what he hears, and he will tell you
what is yet to come."

JOHN 16:13

You guide me with your counsel, LORD,
   and afterward you will take me into glory.

PSALM 73:24

GUIDANCE

*Keep your father's commands
  and do not forsake your mother's teaching.
Bind them upon your heart forever;
  fasten them around your neck.
When you walk, they will guide you;
  when you sleep, they will watch over you;
  when you awake, they will speak to you.
For these commands are a lamp,
  this teaching is a light,
and the corrections of discipline
  are the way to life.*

PROVERBS 6:20-23

*If I rise on the wings of the dawn,
  if I settle on the far side of the sea,
even there your hand will guide me, LORD,
  your right hand will hold me fast.
If I say, "Surely the darkness will hide me
  and the light become night around me,"
even the darkness will not be dark to you;
  the night will shine like the day,
  for darkness is as light to you.*

PSALM 139:9-12

71

God's Words of Life on

GUIDANCE

Send forth your light and your truth, LORD,
let them guide me;
let them bring me to your holy mountain,
to the place where you dwell.

PSALM 43:3

Good and upright is the LORD;
therefore he instructs sinners in his ways.
He guides the humble in what is right
and teaches them his way.
All the ways of the LORD are loving and faithful
for those who keep the demands of his
covenant.

PSALM 25:8-10

In your unfailing love you will lead
the people you have redeemed, O LORD.
In your strength you will guide them
to your holy dwelling.

EXODUS 15:13

God's Words of Life on
GUIDANCE

Direct me in the path of your commands, LORD,
for there I find delight.
Turn my heart toward your statutes
and not toward selfish gain.
Turn my eyes away from worthless things;
preserve my life according to your word.

PSALM 119:35-37

Show me your ways, O LORD,
teach me your paths;
guide me in your truth and teach me,
for you are God my Savior,
and my hope is in you all day long.

PSALM 25:4-5

This is what the LORD says—
your Redeemer, the Holy One of Israel:
"I am the LORD your God,
who teaches you what is best for you,
who directs you in the way you should go."

ISAIAH 48:17

God's Words of Life on

GUIDANCE

This is what the LORD says:
"Stand at the crossroads and look;
ask for the ancient paths,
ask where the good way is, and walk in it,
and you will find rest for your souls."

JEREMIAH 6:16

"I will give you shepherds after my own heart, who
will lead you with knowledge and understanding,"
says the LORD.

JEREMIAH 3:15

Let the morning bring me word of your unfailing love,
for I have put my trust in you, O LORD.
Show me the way I should go,
for to you I lift up my soul.

PSALM 143:8

Since you are my rock and my fortress, O God,
for the sake of your name lead and guide me.

PSALM 31:3

Devotional Thought on Guidance
MAKING THE RIGHT CHOICE

You make decisions every single day. They can be as small as what you're going to wear that day or as big as choosing to change careers. The story of Abraham's servant, Eliezer, and his search for a wife for Isaac shows how God will guide you in every decision you make, if you'll only ask.

Eliezer doesn't leave the choice of a wife to chance or to which woman looks the best. Instead he commits the decisions to God. Without hesitation, Eliezer goes to God for direction in completing his important task.

Rebekah's immediate decision to follow Eliezer back to his master's home, to travel to a land she has never seen, to marry a man she hasn't met, show her eagerness to follow the Lord's leading. She too is a beautiful example of submission to God's direction.

And God honors both Eliezer and Rebekah for their reliance on him, just as he has promised to honor ours if we approach him in faith (Psalm 17:6).

Whatever decisions you may face today, take them to God and he will guide you to make the very best choice.

God's Words of Life on

HARD TIMES

For Christ's sake, I delight in weaknesses, in insults, in hardships, in persecutions, in difficulties. For when I am weak, then I am strong.

2 CORINTHIANS 12:10

The LORD is a refuge for the oppressed,
a stronghold in times of trouble.

PSALM 9:9

If you are insulted because of the name of Christ, you are blessed, for the Spirit of glory and of God rests on you. ... If you suffer as a Christian, do not be ashamed, but praise God that you bear that name.

1 PETER 4:14, 16

[Trials] have come so that your faith-of greater worth than gold, which perishes even though refined by fire—may be proved genuine and may result in praise, glory and honor when Jesus Christ is revealed.

1 PETER 1:7

HARD TIMES

Consider it pure joy ... whenever you face trials of many kinds, because you know that the testing of your faith develops perseverance. Perseverance must finish its work so that you may be mature and complete, not lacking anything.

JAMES 1:2-4

This I call to mind
and therefore I have hope:
Because of the LORD's great love we are not consumed,
for his compassions never fail.
They are new every morning;
great is your faithfulness.
I say to myself, "The LORD is my portion;
therefore I will wait for him."
The LORD is good to those whose hope is in him,
to the one who seeks him;
it is good to wait quietly
for the salvation of the LORD.

LAMENTATIONS 3:21-26

God's Words of Life on

HARD TIMES

Endure hardship as discipline. ... No discipline seems pleasant at the time, but painful. Later on, however, it produces a harvest of righteousness and peace for those who have been trained by it.

HEBREWS 12:7, 11

Who shall separate us from the love of Christ? Shall trouble or hardship or persecution or famine or nakedness or danger or sword? ... No, in all these things we are more than conquerors through him who loved us.

ROMANS 8:35, 37

We say with confidence,
"The Lord is my helper;
*   I will not be afraid.*
What can man do to me?"

HEBREWS 13:6

Because Jesus himself suffered when he was tempted, he is able to help those who are being tempted.

HEBREWS 2:18

God's Words of Life on

HARD TIMES

Our struggle is not against flesh and blood, but against the rulers, against the authorities, against the powers of this dark world and against the spiritual forces of evil in the heavenly realms. Therefore put on the full armor of God, so that when the day of evil comes, you may be able to stand your ground, and after you have done everything, to stand. Stand firm then, with the belt of truth buckled around your waist, with the breastplate of righteousness in place, and with your feet fitted with the readiness that comes from the gospel of peace. In addition to all this, take up the shield of faith, with which you can extinguish all the flaming arrows of the evil one. Take the helmet of salvation and the sword of the Spirit, which is the word of God.

EPHESIANS 6:12-17

*God has not despised or disdained
    the suffering of the afflicted one;
he has not hidden his face from him
    but has listened to his cry for help.*

PSALM 22:24

HARD TIMES

With your help I can advance against a troop;
  with my God I can scale a wall.

PSALM 18:29

In my alarm I said,
  "I am cut off from your sight!"
Yet you heard my cry for mercy
  when I called to you for help, O LORD.

PSALM 31:22

I waited patiently for the LORD;
  he turned to me and heard my cry.
He lifted me out of the slimy pit,
  out of the mud and mire;
he set my feet on a rock
  and gave me a firm place to stand.
He put a new song in my mouth,
  a hymn of praise to our God.

PSALM 40:1-3

WHEN YOU ARE WEAK, HE IS STRONG

It's a foggy place, a place of dark uncertainty. You slide farther and farther down, but you're helpless to stop the descent. You'd love to climb up and out of this pit, but at this point just stopping the fall would be enough. You look at the past and see what you've lost, but you don't know how to get it back. You're discouraged, heavy, hopeless and alone. You wonder where God is. Why does he seem so far away?

In a time of prayer confess your need for God. Be honest with him. The Holy Spirit can bring hope and peace to your heart. Your struggle may be caused by physical, emotional or spiritual fatigue. Maybe you feel that your resources have all been drained.

In every aspect of your life, God's grace is sufficient (2 Corinthians 12:9). This is a deep truth that you can use again and again in your heart and in your life. It is when you are struggling, when you are weak, that God is strong in you (1 Corinthians 1:27-31). Your weakness is God's cue to step in and help.

God's Words of Life on
HEALING

Praise the LORD, O my soul,
 and forget not all his benefits—
who forgives all your sins
 and heals all your diseases,
who redeems your life from the pit
 and crowns you with love and compassion,
who satisfies your desires with good things
 so that your youth is renewed like the eagle's.

PSALM 103:2-5

God heals the brokenhearted
 and binds up their wounds.

PSALM 147:3

[The Messiah] was pierced for our transgressions,
 he was crushed for our iniquities;
the punishment that brought us peace was upon him,
 and by his wounds we are healed.

ISAIAH 53:5

HEALING

Heal me, O LORD, and I will be healed;
save me and I will be saved,
for you are the one I praise.

JEREMIAH 17:14

Jesus himself bore our sins in his body on the tree, so that
we might die to sins and live for righteousness; by his
wounds you have been healed.

1 PETER 2:24

Is any one of you sick? He should call the elders of
the church to pray over him and anoint him with oil
in the name of the Lord. And the prayer offered in
faith will make the sick person well; the Lord will
raise him up. If he has sinned, he will be forgiven.
Therefore confess your sins to each other and pray
for each other so that you may be healed. The prayer
of a righteous man is powerful and effective.

JAMES 5:14-16

God's Words of Life on

HEALING

"For you who revere my name, the sun of righteous-ness will rise with healing in its wings," says the
LORD.

MALACHI 4:2

Blessed is he who has regard for the weak;
the LORD *delivers him in times of trouble.*
The LORD *will protect him and preserve his life. ...*
The LORD *will sustain him on his sickbed*
and restore him from his bed of illness.

PSALM 41:1-3

Restore us, O God;
make your face shine upon us,
that we may be saved.

PSALM 80:3

The God of all grace, who called you to his eternal
glory in Christ, after you have suffered a little while,
will himself restore you and make you strong, firm
and steadfast.

1 PETER 5:10

NOT WHAT YOU EXPECT

In John 9:1-7 we read the story of a miraculous healing that Jesus performed. Jesus already has the reputation for being a miracle worker. He heals the sick, usually with a touch or a word. But Jesus does the unexpected to a blind man in this passage. He spits on the ground, makes mud pie and puts it on the man's eyes. Then he tells the man to go to the Pool of Siloam and wash away the mud. Suppose the man had said, "Ugh! That's disgusting! I'm not going to embarrass myself by walking through town with this mud made with spittle on my face!" Do you think he would have been healed anyway?

Sometimes God comes in unexpected ways. Sometimes God does things that seem totally unlike the way you think he should act. God may even allow sickness or hurt to come into your life to help you learn to love him more. At these times, when even our own health is out of our control, we can learn to turn to God and lean on him. He *is* in control and will bring you healing in his perfect timing.

The next time you find yourself in need of healing, remember that God may be trying to teach you something. Wait and listen for his voice. He will surely bring comfort, healing, and a fresh, new perspective on his love.

HEAVEN

I saw the Holy City, the new Jerusalem, coming down out of heaven from God, prepared as a bride beautifully dressed for her husband. And I heard a loud voice from the throne saying, "Now the dwelling of God is with men, and he will live with them. They will be his people, and God himself will be with them and be their God. He will wipe every tear from their eyes. There will be no more death or mourning or crying or pain, for the old order of things has passed away."

He who was seated on the throne said, "I am making everything new!" Then he said, "Write this down, for these words are trustworthy and true."

He said to me: "It is done. I am the Alpha and the Omega, the Beginning and the End. To him who is thirsty I will give to drink without cost from the spring of the water of life."

REVELATION 21:2-6

In keeping with his promise we are looking forward to a new heaven and a new earth, the home of righteousness.

2 PETER 3:13

HEAVEN

*We believe that Jesus died and rose again and so we
believe that God will bring with Jesus those who
have fallen asleep in him. According to the Lord's
own word, we tell you that we who are still alive,
who are left till the coming of the Lord, will certainly not precede those who have fallen asleep. For
the Lord himself will come down from heaven, with
a loud command, with the voice of the archangel
and with the trumpet call of God, and the dead in
Christ will rise first. After that, we who are still alive
and are left will be caught up together with them in
the clouds to meet the Lord in the air. And so we will
be with the Lord forever.*

1 THESSALONIANS 4:14-17

*[The angel] carried me away in the Spirit to a moun-
tain great and high, and showed me the Holy City,
Jerusalem, coming down out of heaven from God. It
shone with the glory of God, and its brilliance was
like that of a very precious jewel, like a jasper, clear
as crystal.*

REVELATION 21:10-11

HEAVEN

The Lord will rescue me from every evil attack and will bring me safely to his heavenly kingdom.

2 TIMOTHY 4:18

Our citizenship is in heaven. And we eagerly await a Savior from there, the Lord Jesus Christ.

PHILIPPIANS 3:20

God raised us up with Christ and seated us with him in the heavenly realms in Christ Jesus, in order that in the coming ages he might show the incomparable riches of his grace, expressed in his kindness to us in Christ Jesus.

EPHESIANS 2:6-7

Our light and momentary troubles are achieving for us an eternal glory that far outweighs them all. So we fix our eyes not on what is seen, but on what is unseen. For what is seen is temporary, but what is unseen is eternal.

2 CORINTHIANS 4:17-18

God's Words of Life on

HEAVEN

"*Rejoice that your names are written in heaven.*"

LUKE 10:20

Your word, O LORD, is eternal;
*   it stands firm in the heavens.*
Your faithfulness continues through all generations;
*   you established the earth, and it endures.*

PSALM 119:89-90

Jesus said, "Blessed are you when men hate you,
when they exclude you and insult you and reject
your name as evil, because of the Son of Man.
Rejoice in that day and leap for joy, because great is
your reward in heaven."

LUKE 6:22-23

Jesus said, "Let the little children come to me, and
do not hinder them, for the kingdom of heaven
belongs to such as these."

MATTHEW 19:14

God's Words of Life on

HEAVEN

Jesus said, "When the Son of Man comes in his glory, and all the angels with him, he will sit on his throne in heavenly glory. ...

Then the King will say to those on his right, 'Come, you who are blessed by my Father; take your inheritance, the kingdom prepared for you since the creation of the world. For I was hungry and you gave me something to eat, I was thirsty and you gave me something to drink, I was a stranger and you invited me in, I needed clothes and you clothed me, I was sick and you looked after me, I was in prison and you came to visit me.'

"Then the righteous will answer him, 'Lord, when did we see you hungry and feed you, or thirsty and give you something to drink? When did we see you a stranger and invite you in, or needing clothes and clothe you? When did we see you sick or in prison and go to visit you?'

"The King will reply, 'I tell you the truth, whatever you did for one of the least of these brothers of mine, you did for me.'"

MATTHEW 25:31, 34-40

Devotional Thought on Heaven
A TASTE OF HEAVEN

A kingdom is the reign or the realm of a king. The kingdom of heaven is the royal reign—kingship—of Jesus Christ. Wherever Jesus reigns, whether physically or spiritually, the kingdom of heaven exists. Jesus said that his kingdom "is not of this world," but "is from another place" (John 18:36). But the Bible also speaks of the kingdom of heaven here on earth (Matthew 12:28).

Does the state of the world discourage you? Are you tired of struggling with sin? There is hope. You will live in a kingdom of perfection—for all eternity. But even now you may taste that kingdom during times of spiritual communion with Jesus. When you experience and enjoy God, you taste the glory to come.

Time spent in prayer can be a taste of heaven. Sit quietly for a few minutes. Allow the Holy Spirit to refresh you and give you strength. Thank him for your taste of heaven and that you will be with him eternally to know him even better.

God's Words of Life on

HOPE

Even youths grow tired and weary,
*   and young men stumble and fall;*
but those who hope in the LORD
*   will renew their strength.*
They will soar on wings like eagles;
*   they will run and not grow weary,*
*   they will walk and not be faint.*

ISAIAH 40:30-31

"Everything is possible for him who believe."

MARK 9:23

Dear friends, now we are children of God, and what
we will be has not yet been made known. But we
know that when Christ appears, we shall be like
him, for we shall see him as he is. Everyone who has
this hope in him purifies himself, just as he is pure.

1 JOHN 3:2-3

God has delivered us from such a deadly peril, and
he will deliver us. On him we have set our hope that
he will continue to deliver us.

2 CORINTHIANS 1:10

God's Words of Life on

HOPE

The grace of God that brings salvation has appeared to all men. It teaches us to say "No" to ungodliness and worldly passions, and to live self-controlled, upright and godly lives in this present age, while we wait for the blessed hope—the glorious appearing of our great God and Savior, Jesus Christ ...

TITUS 2:11-13

Through Christ you believe in God, who raised him from the dead and glorified him, and so your faith and hope are in God.

1 PETER 1:21

We wait in hope for the LORD;
*   he is our help and our shield.*
In him our hearts rejoice,
*   for we trust in his holy name.*
May your unfailing love rest upon us, O LORD,
*   even as we put our hope in you.*

PSALM 33:20-22

God's Words of Life on

HOPE

We know that in all things God works for the good of those who love him, who have been called according to his purpose. ... What, then, shall we say in response to this? If God is for us, who can be against us?

ROMANS 8:28, 31

May our Lord Jesus Christ himself and God our Father, who loved us and by his grace gave us eternal encouragement and good hope, encourage your hearts and strengthen you in every good deed and word.

2 THESSALONIANS 2:16-17

Praise be to the God and Father of our Lord Jesus Christ! In his great mercy he has given us new birth into a living hope through the resurrection of Jesus Christ from the dead, and into an inheritance that can never perish, spoil or fade—kept in heaven for you, who through faith are shielded by God's power until the coming of the salvation that is ready to be revealed in the last time.

1 PETER 1:3-5

HOPE

When the kindness and love of God our Savior appeared, he saved us, not because of righteous things we had done, but because of his mercy. He saved us through the washing of rebirth and renewal by the Holy Spirit, whom he poured out on us generously through Jesus Christ our Savior, so that, having been justified by his grace, we might become heirs having the hope of eternal life.

TITUS 3:4-7

No one whose hope is in you, LORD,
  will ever be put to shame

PSALM 25:3

Find rest, O my soul, in God alone;
  my hope comes from him.
He alone is my rock and my salvation;
  he is my fortress, I will not be shaken.

PSALM 62:5-6

I will always have hope;
  I will praise you more and more, LORD.

PSALM 71:14

God's Words of Life on

HOPE

~❧~

The LORD delights in those who fear him,
    who put their hope in his unfailing love.

PSALM 147:11

Hope that is seen is no hope at all. Who hopes for
what he already has? But if we hope for what we do
not yet have, we wait for it patiently.

ROMANS 8:24-25

Because God wanted to make the unchanging
nature of his purpose very clear to the heirs of what
was promised, he confirmed it with an oath. God did
this so that, by two unchangeable things in which it
is impossible for God to lie, we who have fled to take
hold of the hope offered to us may be greatly encouraged. We have this hope as an anchor for the soul,
firm and secure.

HEBREWS 6:17-19

May the God of hope fill you with all joy and peace
as you trust in him, so that you may overflow with
hope by the power of the Holy Spirit.

ROMANS 15:13

Devotional Thought on Hope
A LIVING HOPE

She is dying of cancer and the treatment options are exhausted. "I've given up hoping to get well, " she says, "but my hope in the Lord will never die." Her hope to get well has been a wish, a desire, but her hope in the Lord is a firm conviction. God knows you cannot live without hope. He's not in the business of merely fulfilling wishes; he is in the business of giving "a living hope." Even facing death, Christians, though at times discouraged, have a living, eternal hope.

Where does this hope come from? Just as faith is a gift of God, hope is as well. It is God's sweet kiss of mercy when you are born into his family (1 Peter 1:3-4). This hope is based on God's unfailing love and your full redemption through Christ. God himself guards this gift for you in heaven.

If you are experiencing a lack of hope, believe that God "will make the Valley of [Trouble] a door of hope" (Hosea 2:15). God will take your trouble and turn it into an entry for hope and a doorway to him.

In a time of prayer, picture yourself handing your worries and despair to Jesus. See yourself walking through a doorway toward Jesus. Allow the Holy Spirit to fill you with a "living hope."

God's Words of Life on
IDENTITY

We are God's workmanship, created in Christ Jesus to do good works, which God prepared in advance for us to do.

EPHESIANS 2:10

Know that the LORD is God.
>   It is he who made us, and we are his;
>   we are his people, the sheep of his pasture.

PSALM 100:3

When Christ, who is your life, appears, then you also will appear with him in glory.

COLOSSIANS 3:4

What is man that you are mindful of him, O LORD,
>   the son of man that you care for him?
You made him a little lower than the heavenly beings
>   and crowned him with glory and honor.
You made him ruler over the works of your hands;
>   you put everything under his feet.

PSALM 8:4-6

IDENTITY

Jesus said, "Are not five sparrows sold for two pennies? Yet not one of them is forgotten by God. Indeed, the very hairs of your head are all numbered. Don't be afraid; you are worth more than many sparrows."

LUKE 12:6-7

How great is the love the Father has lavished on us, that we should be called children of God! And that is what we are!

1 JOHN 3:1

"I will be a Father to you, and you will be my sons and daughters," says the Lord Almighty.

2 CORINTHIANS 6:18

We are God's fellow workers; you are God's field, God's building.

1 CORINTHIANS 3:9

God's Words of Life on

IDENTITY

The Spirit himself testifies with our spirit that we are God's children. Now if we are children, then we are heirs—heirs of God and co-heirs with Christ, if indeed we share in his sufferings in order that we may also share in his glory.

ROMANS 8:16-17

Just as each of us has one body with many members, and these members do not all have the same function, so in Christ we who are many form one body, and each member belongs top all the others.

ROMANS 12:4-5

"See, I have engraved you on the palms of my hands," says the LORD.

ISAIAH 49:16

So God created man in his own image, in the image of God he created him; male and female he created them.

GENESIS 1:27

IDENTITY

You created my inmost being;
*   you knit me together in my mother's womb.*
I praise you because I am fearfully
*   and wonderfully made;*
*   your works are wonderful,*
*   I know that full well.*

PSALM 139:13-14

We are the temple of the living God. As God
has said: "I will live with them and walk among
them, and I will be their God, and they will be
my people."

2 CORINTHIANS 6:16

In God we live and move and have our being.

ACTS 17:28

You have been born again, not of perishable seed,
but of imperishable, through the living and enduring
word of God.

1 PETER 1:23

God's Words of Life on

IDENTITY

"Fear not, for I have redeemed you;
    I have summoned you by name; you are mine,"
        says the LORD.

ISAIAH 43:1

From the beginning God chose you to be saved
through the sanctifying work of the Spirit and
through belief in the truth.

2 THESSALONIANS 2:13

As you come to him, the living Stone—rejected by
men but chosen by God and precious to him—you
also, like living stones, are being built into a spiritual
house to be a holy priesthood, offering spiritual sacri-
fices acceptable to God through Jesus Christ.

1 PETER 2:4-5

The LORD your God is with you,
    he is mighty to save.
He will take great delight in you,
    he will quiet you with his love
he will rejoice over you with singing.

ZEPHANIAH 3:17

THE GOD WHO SINGS

Imagine hearing God sing. Does it sound like the mighty roar of thunder or like a soft, gentle whisper? It is powerful and strong, yet unimaginably beautiful, pure and sweet. And he is singing that glorious song over you! Why does God sing over you? Because he delights in you! You make his heart sing with joy!

Do you believe this? If not, why not? There are obstacles, you say—your sin and guilt, your constant wandering from God, and your fear of rejection. Yes, you are a sinner. That is the very reason for you to go to God. God will never reject you when you come to him. He will never forsake you.

God's love for you is deep and strong. It will never be shaken. When you take a step of faith and trust in God's love for you, you will discover that he is singing over you from a heart bursting with joy and pride. He is your loving Father. Listen to the special love song he is singing just for you.

God's Words of Life on

JOY

Our mouths were filled with laughter,
  our tongues with songs of joy.
Then it was said among the nations,
  "The LORD has done great things for them."
The LORD has done great things for us,
  and we are filled with joy.

PSALM 126:2-3

The LORD is my strength and my shield;
  my heart trusts in him, and I am helped.
My heart leaps for joy
  and I will give thanks to him in song.

PSALM 28:7

Those living far away fear your wonders, O LORD;
  where morning dawns and evening fades
  you call forth songs of joy.

PSALM 65:8

God's Words of Life on

JOY

Jesus said, "As the Father has loved me, so have I loved you. Now remain in my love. If you obey my commands, you will remain in my love, just as I have obeyed my Father's commands and remain in his love. I have told you this so that my joy may be in you and that your joy may be complete."

JOHN 15:9-11

Satisfy us in the morning with your unfailing love,
O LORD,
       that we may sing for joy and be glad all our days.

PSALM 90:14

       The ransomed of the LORD will return.
They will enter Zion with singing;
       everlasting joy will crown their heads.
Gladness and joy will overtake them,
       and sorrow and sighing will flee away.

ISAIAH 35:10

JOY

*May the God of hope fill you with all joy and peace
as you trust in him, so that you may overflow with
hope by the power of the Holy Spirit.*

ROMANS 15:13

*You have made known to me the path of life, O LORD;
    you will fill me with joy in your presence,
    with eternal pleasures at your right hand.*

PSALM 16:11

*Let all who take refuge in you be glad;
    let them ever sing for joy.
Spread your protection over them,
    that those who love your name may rejoice in you.
For surely, O LORD, you bless the righteous;
    you surround them with your favor
    as with a shield.*

PSALM 5:11-12

God's Words of Life on

JOY

When I said, "My foot is slipping,"
    your love, O LORD, supported me.
When anxiety was great within me,
    your consolation brought joy to my soul.

PSALM 94:18-19

The joy of the LORD is your strength.

NEHEMIAH 8:10

Though you have not seen Jesus, you love him; and even though you do not see him now, you believe in him and are filled with an inexpressible and glorious joy, for you are receiving the goal of your faith, the salvation of your souls.

1 PETER 1:8-9

Jesus said, "Until now you have not asked for anything in my name. Ask and you will receive, and your joy will be complete."

JOHN 16:24

God's Words of Life on

JOY

⌘

When your words came, I ate them;
*   they were my joy and my heart's delight,*
for I bear your name,
*   O LORD God Almighty.*

JEREMIAH 15:16

You will go out in joy
*   and be led forth in peace;*
the mountains and hills
*   will burst into song before you,*
and all the trees of the field
*   will clap their hands.*

ISAIAH 55:12

To God who is able to keep you from falling and to
present you before his glorious presence without fault
and with great joy—to the only God our Savior be
glory, majesty, power and authority, through Jesus
Christ our Lord, before all ages, now and forever-
more! Amen.

JUDE 24-25

JOY, COME WHAT MAY

The struggles and tragedies of this life need not affect your joy as a child of God. True joy is based on the spiritual realities of who God is and what he has promised. God is good and God is faithful—regardless of your situation.

Read 1 Chronicles 16:8-12, 23-26. This beautiful psalm of praise expresses the unique joy that belongs to a child of God. You have no need to fear or to be anxious. Your God is powerful and mighty to save (Zephaniah 3:17). Despite your circumstances you can "glory in his holy name" and your heart can rejoice as you seek him and the strength he offers.

Is your heart bursting with joy today? Give thanks! Speak aloud your joy and thanksgiving to God. Spend time praising and worshiping him through music and prayer. He is worthy of your exuberant praise. If you are longing for this kind of joy, ask the Holy Spirit to fill you. The Spirit is the joy-bringer. "Ask and you will receive, and your joy will be complete" (John 16:24). That's a promise from Jesus' own lips, and he is faithful.

God's Words of Life on

LISTENING

*I will listen to what God the LORD will say;
    he promises peace to his people, his saints.*

PSALM 85:8

*Jesus said, "The seed on good soil stands for those
with a noble and good heart, who hear the word,
retain it, and by persevering produce a crop."*

LUKE 8:15

*He who listens to a life-giving rebuke
    will be at home among the wise.*

PROVERBS 15:31

*Pay attention and listen to the sayings of the wise;
    apply your heart to what I teach,
for it is pleasing when you keep them in your heart
    and have all of them ready on your lips.
So that your trust may be in the LORD,
    I teach you today, even you.*

PROVERBS 22:17-19

LISTENING

Jesus said, *"Everyone who listens to the Father and learns from him comes to me."*

JOHN 6:45

The Sovereign LORD has given me an instructed tongue,
*   to know the word that sustains the weary.*
He wakens me morning by morning,
*   wakens my ear to listen like one being taught.*

ISAIAH 50:4

Anyone who listens to the word but does not do what it says is like a man who looks at his face in a mirror and, after looking at himself, goes away and immediately forgets what he looks like. But the man who looks intently into the perfect law that gives freedom, and continues to do this, not forgetting what he has heard, but doing it—he will be blessed in what he does.

JAMES 1:23-25

God's Words of Life on
LISTENING

Jesus said, "My sheep listen to my voice; I know them, and they follow me. I give them eternal life, and they shall never perish; no one can snatch them out of my hand. My Father, who has given them to me, is greater than all; no one can snatch them out of my Father's hand. I and the Father are one."

JOHN 10:27-30

Listen to advice and accept instruction, and in the end you will be wise.

PROVERBS 19:20

Paul wrote, what you heard from me, keep as the pattern of sounding teaching, with faith and love in Christ Jesus.

2 TIMOTHY 1:13

Faith comes from hearing the message, and the message is heard through the word of Christ

ROMANS 10:17

Devotional Thought on Listening
THE VOICE OF GOD

Imagine actually hearing the voice of God! Moses seems to accept this as a normal occurrence. The words "the LORD said to Moses" appear 138 times in the Old Testament! God wasn't silent then, and he's not silent today. Even though he might not speak audibly, God still has much to say to us.

The Bible is the chief way the Spirit speaks and is the test for all the other voices that claim to be God's. It is "living and active" (Hebrews 4:12). It tells us who God is and who we are.

God is a person. He wants to have a relationship with you. A good relationship requires communication. In other words, he may be speaking, but are you listening?

During your prayer time, listen for the Lord to speak to your heart, perhaps through a Bible verse, a song, a mental impression or a reaction of some kind. The Spirit speaks to the core of your being, filling that deep place in you—that place no one else can reach.

God's Words of Life on

LOVE

Love is patient, love is kind. It does not envy, it does not boast, it is not proud. It is not rude, it is not self-seeking. It is not easily angered, it keeps no record of wrongs. Love does not delight in evil but rejoices with the truth. It always protects, always trusts, always hopes, always perseveres. Love never fails.

1 CORINTHIANS 13:4-8

The LORD loves righteousness and justice;
    the earth is full of his unfailing love.

PSALM 33:5

"God so loved the world that he gave his one and only Son, that whoever believes in him shall not perish but have eternal life."

JOHN 3:16

How great is the love the Father has lavished on us, that we should be called children of God! And that is what we are!

1 JOHN 3:1

God's Words of Life on

LOVE

As God's chosen people, holy and dearly loved, clothe yourselves with compassion, kindness, humility, gentleness and patience. Bear with each other and forgive whatever grievances you may have against one another. Forgive as the Lord forgave you. And over all these virtues put on love, which binds them all together in perfect unity.

COLOSSIANS 3:12-14

We know and rely on the love God has for us. God is love. Whoever lives in love lives in God, and God in him.

1 JOHN 4:16

*I will praise you, O LORD, among the nations;
     I will sing of you among the peoples.
For great is your love, reaching to the heavens;
     your faithfulness reaches to the skies.*

PSALM 57:9-10

He who covers over an offense promotes love.

PROVERBS 17:9

God's Words of Life on

LOVE

God has poured out his love into our hearts by the Holy Spirit, whom he has given us. ... God demonstrates his own love for us in this: While we were still sinners, Christ died for us.

ROMANS 5:5, 8

Dear friends, let us love one another, for love comes from God. Everyone who loves has been born of God and knows God.

1 JOHN 4:7

*I trust in your unfailing love, O LORD;
    my heart rejoices in your salvation.
I will sing to the LORD,
    for he has been good to me.*

PSALM 13:5-6

"Greater love has no one than this, that he lay down his life for his friends."

JOHN 15:13

God's Words of Life on

LOVE

Because of the LORD'S great love we are not consumed,
for his compassions never fail.
They are new every morning;
great is your faithfulness.

LAMENTATIONS 3:22-23

There is no fear in love. But perfect love drives out
fear.

1 JOHN 4:18

I pray that you, being rooted and established in love,
may have power, together with all the saints, to
grasp how wide and long and high and deep is the
love of Christ, and to know this love that surpasses
knowledge—that you may be filled to the measure
of all the fullness of God.

EPHESIANS 3:17-19

Jesus said, "Love one another. As I have loved you,
so you must love one another. By this all men will
know that you are my disciples, if you love one
another."

JOHN 13:34-35

God's Words of Life on

LOVE

We love because God first loved us.

1 JOHN 4:19

*This is love: not that we loved God, but that he
loved us and sent his Son as an atoning sacrifice for
our sins.*

1 JOHN 4:10

*God did not give us a spirit of timidity, but a spirit of
power, of love and of self-discipline.*

2 TIMOTHY 1:7

*Those who plan what is good find love and
faithfulness.*

PROVERBS 14:22

*The LORD is gracious and compassionate,
     slow to anger and rich in love.
The LORD is good to all;
     he has compassion on all he has made.*

PSALM 145:8-9

GOD'S RIVER OF DELIGHTS

In Psalm 36:5-9, David speaks of a river flowing with God's delights. God's river of delights is flowing out to you. God wants to satisfy your needs and your desires. His love is boundless, reaching to the heavens; it is priceless and unfailing. God is offering you a drink—a taste of all that he desires to lavish on you.

The prophet Ezekiel also speaks of a river (Ezekiel 47:1-12). Notice that Ezekiel enters the water where it is ankle-deep. As he is led farther into the water, it becomes knee-deep, then waist-deep, then deep enough to swim in—"a river that no one could cross" (Ezekiel 47:5). When God invites you into his presence, you enter slowly; you experience his glory, but it does not overwhelm you. As your trust in God and your desire for more of him increases, he leads you deeper into his glory until you are surrounded by his presence.

As you pray this week, meditate on God's love for you. As you quiet yourself in awareness of his presence, give the Holy Spirit freedom to speak to your heart. When you delight in God, your deepest desires are met in him. When you delight in God, he delights in you (Psalm 147:11).

God's Words of Life on

MONEY

I know what it is to be in need, and I know what it is to have plenty. I have learned the secret of being content in any and every situation, whether well fed or hungry, whether living in plenty or in want. I can do everything through Christ who gives me strength.

PHILIPPIANS 4:12-13

He who gathers money little by little makes it grow.

PROVERBS 13:11

Jesus sat down opposite the place where the offerings were put and watched the crowd putting their money into the temple treasury. Many rich people threw in large amounts. But a poor widow came and put in two very small copper coins, worth only a fraction of a penny. Calling his disciples to him, Jesus said, "I tell you the truth, this poor widow has put more into the treasury than all the others. They all gave out of their wealth; but she, out of her poverty, put in everything—all she had to live on."

MARK 12:41-44

God's Words of Life on

MONEY

Keep your lives free from the love of money and be content with what you have, because God has said, "Never will I leave you; never will I forsake you." So we say with confidence, "The Lord is my helper; I will not be afraid. What can man do to me?"

HEBREWS 13:5-6

Remember this: Whoever sows sparingly will also reap sparingly, and whoever sows generously will also reap generously. Each man should give what he has decided in his heart to give, not reluctantly or under compulsion, for God loves a cheerful giver. And God is able to make all grace abound to you, so that in all things at all times, having all that you need, you will abound in every good work.

2 CORINTHIANS 9:6-8

God's Words of Life on

MONEY

"It is more blessed to give than to receive."

ACTS 20:35

God who supplies seed to the sower and bread for food will also supply and increase your store of seed and will enlarge the harvest of your righteousness. You will be made rich in every way so that you can be generous on every occasion, and ... your generosity will result in thanksgiving to God.

2 CORINTHIANS 9:10-11

Good will come to him who is generous and lends freely, who conducts his affairs with justice.

PSALM 112:5

"Bring the whole tithe into the storehouse, that there may be food in my house. Test me in this," says the LORD *Almighty, "and see if I will not throw open the floodgates of heaven and pour out so much blessing that you will not have room enough for it."*

MALACHI 3:10

LESS IS MORE

In Mark 12:41-44 Jesus watches the temple crowd as people give their offerings. He hears—everyone can—the sound of the precious metals dropping into the temple treasury. Yet he doesn't take much notice of the coins. He is intent on the people's hearts. The rich give plenty, and Jesus nods. It is good they do so out of their abundance. Then he sees a peasant widow who gives from her scarcity. She gives two coins worth less than a penny. These are the smallest of coins, equal to about one-eighth of a cent.

Contrary to all human reasoning, the Savior commends her. The woman is stretching herself, even denying herself. And Jesus sees her heart. The widow knows that her source of provision is not the coins. Her source is God. She gives all, confident that he will provide. In Jesus' eyes, her less is more. So is yours. Whatever you give from the heart is big in God's eyes.

God's Words of Life on

OBEDIENCE

This is love for God: to obey his commands. And his commands are not burdensome, for everyone born of God overcomes the world.

1 JOHN 5:3-4

I will always obey your law, LORD,
*   for ever and ever.*
I will walk about in freedom,
*   for I have sought out your precepts.*

PSALM 119:44-45

Jesus said, "As the Father has loved me, so have I loved you. Now remain in my love. If you obey my commands, you will remain in my love, just as I have obeyed my Father's commands and remain in his love. I have told you this so that my joy may be in you and that your joy may be complete."

JOHN 15:9-11

God's Words of Life on
OBEDIENCE

Children, obey your parents in the Lord, for this is right. "Honor your father and mother"—which is the first commandment with a promise—"that it may go well with you and that you may enjoy long life on the earth."

EPHESIANS 6:1-3

He who obeys instructions guards his life.

PROVERBS 19:16

Jesus said, "If anyone loves me, he will obey my teaching. My Father will love him, and we will come to him and make our home with him."

JOHN 14:23

Your statutes are wonderful, LORD;
    therefore I obey them.
The unfolding of your words gives light;
    it gives understanding to the simple.

PSALM 119:129-130

God's Words of Life on
OBEDIENCE

*If anyone obeys his word, God's love is truly made
complete in him.*

1 JOHN 2:5

*From everlasting to everlasting
the LORD's love is with those who fear him,
and his righteousness with their
children's children—
with those who keep his covenant
and remember to obey his precepts.*

PSALM 103:17-18

*All these blessings will come upon you and accompany you if you obey the LORD your God: You will
be blessed in the city and blessed in the country. The
fruit of your womb will be blessed, and the crops of
your land and the young of your livestock—the
calves of your herds and the lambs of your flocks.
Your basket and your kneading trough will be
blessed. You will be blessed when you come in and
blessed when you go out.*

DEUTERONOMY 28:2-6

126

WHOSE SLAVE ARE YOU?

Have you become a slave to your job, your home, your spouse, your children? Eventually, something or someone will run your life. The truth is that all of us are slaves, either "slaves to sin" or "slaves to righteousness" (Romans 6:16-18).

In Romans 8:9-17 there is wonderful news about our "slave status." Although you were once a slave controlled by your sinful nature, you are now free to be controlled by the Holy Spirit, if you have accepted Christ. Jesus no longer calls you a servant he calls you his friend (John 15:14-15). God has given you his Spirit, "and where the Spirit of the Lord is, there is freedom" (2 Corinthians 3:17). You now have the freedom to serve and obey God (Ephesians 6:6) and to "serve one another in love" (Galatians 5:13).

Examine your heart. Are you living a life controlled by self, by sin, or by the Spirit? Ask God to reveal areas in your life that need to be surrendered to his control. Pray for the Holy Spirit's power to choose God's way and God's will in your life. In obedience to him you will find true freedom to enjoy both God and your life.

PATIENCE

Be patient, ... until the Lord's coming. See how the farmer waits for the land to yield its valuable crop and how patient he is for the autumn and spring rains. Be patient and stand firm, because the Lord's coming is near.

JAMES 5:7-8

Love is patient.

1 CORINTHIANS 13:4

I waited patiently for the LORD;
he turned to me and heard my cry.

PSALM 40:1

The Lord is not slow in keeping his promise, as some understand slowness. He is patient with you, not wanting anyone to perish, but everyone to come to repentance.

2 PETER 3:9

God's Words of Life on

PATIENCE

The end of a matter is better than its beginning, and patience is better than pride.

ECCLESIASTES 7:8

A patient man has great understanding.

PROVERBS 14:29

Be joyful in hope, patient in affliction, faithful in prayer.

ROMANS 12:12

The fruit of the Spirit is love, joy, peace, patience, kindness, goodness, faithfulness, gentleness and self-control.

GALATIANS 5:22-23

Be completely humble and gentle; be patient, bearing with one another in love. Make every effort to keep the unity of the Spirit through the bond of peace.

EPHESIANS 4:2-3

God's Words of Life on

PATIENCE

We pray ... that you may live a life worthy of the Lord and may please him in every way: bearing fruit in every good work, growing in the knowledge of God, being strengthened with all power according to his glorious might so that you may have great endurance and patience, and joyfully giving thanks to the Father.

COLOSSIANS 1:10-12

As God's chosen people, holy and dearly loved, clothe yourselves with compassion, kindness, humility, gentleness and patience.

COLOSSIANS 3:12

Bear in mind that our Lord's patience means salvation.

2 PETER 3:15

Jesus said, "Since you have kept my command to endure patiently, I will also keep you from the hour of trial that is going to come upon the whole world to test those who live on the earth."

REVELATION 3:10

Devotional Thought on Patience
GOD'S TIMETABLE

We live in a "give it to me now" culture that is pathological about getting things on demand. With the click of a mouse, we can access information through the Internet, and in a matter of seconds, gather thousands of files of information on every topic—from A through Z. We want it now, or better yet, yesterday!

In a world stuck in fast-forward mode, God wants us to know that he does not work on our timetable. To him a day is like a thousand years and a thousand years are like a day; which is to say, God's timing is very much his own. He is at work— on his schedule. Jesus is coming soon, but what is "soon" in God's timing could be very different from ours. His example of loving patience with those who do not believe reminds us of the importance of patience in our own lives. If Jesus can be patient, even with people who continue to deny him, then we can certainly be patient with the people and situations in our lives.

God's Words of Life on

PEACE

*Jesus said, "Peace I leave with you; my peace I give
you. I do not give to you as the world gives. Do not
let your hearts be troubled and do not be afraid."*

JOHN 14:27

*To us a child is born,
        to us a son is given,
        and the government will be on his shoulders.
And he will be called
        Wonderful Counselor, Mighty God,
        Everlasting Father, Prince of Peace.*

ISAIAH 9:6

*The LORD gives strength to his people;
        the LORD blesses his people with peace.*

PSALM 29:11

*You will keep in perfect peace
        him whose mind is steadfast,
        because he trusts in you, O LORD.*

ISAIAH 26:3

God's Words of Life on

PEACE

"*Be still, and know that I am God.*"

PSALM 46:10

The fruit of righteousness will be peace;
the effect of righteousness will be quietness and
confidence forever.

ISAIAH 32:17

Let the peace of Christ rule in your hearts, since as
members of one body you were called to peace. And
be thankful.

COLOSSIANS 3:15

Great peace have they who love your law, O LORD,
and nothing can make them stumble.

PSALM 119:165

God's Words of Life on

PEACE

Consider the blameless, observe the upright;
there is a future for the man of peace.

PSALM 37:37

How beautiful on the mountains
are the feet of those who bring good news,
who proclaim peace,
who bring good tidings,
who proclaim salvation,
who say to Zion,
"Your God reigns!"

ISAIAH 52:7

I will listen to what God the LORD will say;
he promises peace to his people, his saints.

PSALM 85:8

Those who walk uprightly
enter into peace.

ISAIAH 57:2

God's Words of Life on

PEACE

*"Though the mountains be shaken
    and the hills be removed,
yet my unfailing love for you will not be shaken
    nor my covenant of peace be removed,"
    says the LORD, who has compassion on you.*

ISAIAH 54:10

*LORD, you establish peace for us;
    all that we have accomplished
        you have done for us.*

ISAIAH 26:12

A heart at peace gives life to the body.

PROVERBS 14:30

*Grace, mercy and peace from God the Father and
from Jesus Christ, the Father's Son, will be with us in
truth and love.*

2 JOHN 1:3

*Peacemakers who sow in peace raise a harvest of
righteousness.*

JAMES 3:18

PEACE

May the Lord of peace himself give you peace at all times and in every way.

2 THESSALONIANS 3:16

May God himself, the God of peace, sanctify you through and through. May your whole spirit, soul and body be kept blameless at the coming of our Lord Jesus Christ.

1 THESSALONIANS 5:23

In Christ Jesus you who once were far away have been brought near through the blood of Christ. For he himself is our peace.

EPHESIANS 2:13-14

The mind controlled by the Spirit is life and peace.

ROMANS 8:6

Since we have been justified through faith, we have peace with God through our Lord Jesus Christ.

ROMANS 5:1

JESUS, PRINCE OF PEACE

In a world filled with strife, peace often seems too elusive to even hope for. But Scripture makes it clear that peace is indeed possible. God is a God of peace, and peace comes from him.

The traditional Hebrew understanding of peace included completeness, soundness, and well-being of the total person, which is reflected in their greeting for one another that continues to this day: *Shalom* (the Hebrew word for peace). How can you have this kind of peace?

Peace comes through your relationship with Jesus. It is based on your close friendship with him, on consistent—steadfast—time spent with him, on your acceptance of his discipline and, most important, on your trusting in him.

Are you embroiled in strife? Does life always seem turbulent? Peace will come when you embrace the presence of God in your life. Jesus is the Prince of Peace. He has promised to meet your needs, shelter you, and rescue you. Trust him. He is always with you. In the midst of turmoil, do your best to turn your eyes to him. "And the peace of God which transcends all understanding, will guard your hearts and your minds in Christ Jesus" (Philippians 4:7).

God's Words of Life on

PERSEVERANCE

You need to persevere so that when you have done the will of God, you will receive what he has promised.

HEBREWS 10:36

The testing of your faith develops perseverance. Perseverance must finish its work so that you may be mature and complete, not lacking anything.

JAMES 1:3-4

Love always protects, always trusts, always hopes, always perseveres.

1 CORINTHIANS 13:7

Blessed is the man who perseveres under trial, because when he has stood the test, he will receive the crown of life that God has promised to those who love him.

JAMES 1:12

PERSEVERANCE

Since we are surrounded by such a great cloud of witnesses, let us throw off everything that hinders and the sin that so easily entangles, and let us run with perseverance the race marked out for us. Let us fix our eyes on Jesus, the author and perfecter of our faith, who for the joy set before him endured the cross, scorning its shame, and sat down at the right hand of the throne of God. Consider him who endured such opposition from sinful men, so that you will not grow weary and lose heart.

HEBREWS 12:1-3

We consider blessed those who have persevered. You have heard of Job's perseverance and have seen what the Lord finally brought about. The Lord is full of compassion and mercy.

JAMES 5:11

Let us not become weary in doing good, for at the proper time we will reap a harvest if we do not give up.

GALATIANS 6:9

God's Words of Life on

PERSEVERANCE

Make every effort to add to your faith goodness; and to goodness, knowledge; and to knowledge, self-control; and to self-control, perseverance; and to perseverance, godliness; and to godliness, brotherly kindness; and to brotherly kindness, love. For if you possess these qualities in increasing measure, they will keep you from being ineffective and unproductive in your knowledge of our Lord Jesus Christ.

2 PETER 1:5-8

We also rejoice in our sufferings, because we know that suffering produces perseverance; perseverance, character; and character, hope.

ROMANS 5:3-4

May the Lord direct your hearts into God's love and Christ's perseverance.

2 THESSALONIANS 3:5

TROUBLE BRINGS PERSEVERANCE

People are seekers. Often they're seeking the benefits of God—peace, joy, love, and heaven—but they are not seeking the relationship with God required to attain those benefits. God wants people to seek him, not just his benefits. He wants people who are looking for a relationship with him, people who are willing to sacrifice for that relationship—not because he wants to see them suffer but because he knows the benefits suffering brings. Suffering teaches people to be steadfast and determined—to persevere.

Whatever your current circumstances, continue to seek God in the midst of your struggles. He may be allowing you to endure some suffering to develop strength and perseverance in your life. Ask Jesus to help you see your difficulties with a new perspective and to remember that it is eternity that matters.

God's Words of Life on

PRAYER

The Spirit helps us in our weakness. We do not know what we ought to pray for, but the Spirit himself intercedes for us with groans that words cannot express.

ROMANS 8:26

Hear my prayer, O LORD;
*   listen to my cry for mercy.*
In the day of my trouble I will call to you
*   for you will answer me.*

PSALM 86:6-7

"Call to me and I will answer you and tell you great and unsearchable things you do not know," says the LORD.

JEREMIAH 33:3

"When you pray go into your room, close the door and pray to your Father, who is unseen. Then your Father, who sees what is done in secret, will reward you."

MATTHEW 6:6

God's Words of Life on

PRAYER

The prayer offered in faith will make the sick person well; the Lord will raise him up. If he has sinned, he will be forgiven. Therefore confess your sins to each other and pray for each other so that you may be healed. The prayer of a righteous man is powerful and effective.

JAMES 5:15-16

Know that the LORD has set apart the godly for himself;
    The LORD will hear when I call to him.

PSALM 4:3

I called on your name, O LORD,
    from the depths of the pit.
You heard my plea: "Do not close your ears
    to my cry for relief."
You came near when I called you,
    and you said, "Do not fear."

LAMENTATIONS 3:55-57

PRAYER

*I urge ... that requests, prayers, intercession and
thanks-giving be made for everyone—for kings and
all those in authority, that we may live peaceful and
quiet lives in all godliness and holiness.*

1 TIMOTHY 2:1-2

*O LORD, I call to you; come quickly to me.
Hear my voice when I call to you.
May my prayer be set before you like incense;
May the lifting up of my hands
be like the evening sacrifice.*

PSALM 141:1-2

*This is the confidence we have in approaching God:
that if we ask anything according to his will, he
hears us. And if we know that he hears us—whatever we ask—we know that we have what we asked
of him.*

1 JOHN 5:14-15

*If any of you lacks wisdom, he should ask God, who
gives generously to all without finding fault, and it
will be given to him.*

JAMES 1:5

God's Words of Life on

PRAYER

Do not be anxious about anything, but in every-thing, by prayer and petition, with thanksgiving, present your requests to God. And the peace of God, which transcends all understanding, will guard your hearts and your minds in Christ Jesus.

PHILIPPIANS 4:6-7

*In my distress I called to the LORD,
    and he answered me.*

JONAH 2:2

*Listen to my cry for help,
    my King and my God,
    for to you I pray.
In the morning, O LORD, you hear my voice;
    in the morning I lay my requests before you
    and wait in expectation.*

PSALM 5:2-3

*Let everyone who is godly pray to you, LORD,
    while you may be found;
surely when the mighty waters rise,
    they will not reach him.*

PSALM 32:6

God's Words of Life on

PRAYER

God has surely listened
    and heard my voice in prayer.
Praise be to God,
    who has not rejected my prayer
    or withheld his love from me!

PSALM 66:19-20

Jesus said, "This, then, is how you should pray:
'Our Father in heaven,
hallowed be your name,
your kingdom come,
your will be done
    on earth as it is in heaven.
Give us today our daily bread.
Forgive us our debts,
    as we also have forgiven our debtors.
And lead us not into temptation,
but deliver us from the evil one.'"

MATTHEW 6:9-13

GOD HEARS YOUR PRAYERS

Do you ever pray and pray and feel like no one is listening—like your prayers go no farther than the ceiling? Does God hear, even when you feel like he doesn't? Is he always listening? God's Word has much to say about prayer.

Romans 8:26-27 promises that even when you feel you can't adequately express your feelings in words, the Holy Spirit conveys your heart to God.

Jesus makes prayer a high priority during his earthly ministry (Luke 6:12 and Mark 1:35). He takes time late into the night and early in the morning to spend time in prayer without distractions. His example shows us how spending quiet time with God can enrich our walk with the Father.

When you pray, you approach God himself. That knowledge is very humbling. The wonderful result of humility is that God's grace is released (Proverbs 3:34). God desires to hear you and answer you. Go to him in prayer right now. Enjoy God's presence and believe that he hears and will answer you when you call to him (2 Chronicles 7:14; Psalm 6:9).

God's Words of Life on

PROTECTION

Jesus prayed, "I pray for [my disciples]. I am not praying for the world, but for those you have given me, for they are yours. All I have is yours, and all you have is mine. And glory has come to me through them. I will remain in the world no longer, but they are still in the world, and I am coming to you. Holy Father, protect them by the power of your name— the name you gave me—so that they may be one as we are one."

JOHN 17:9-11

Do not withhold your mercy from me, O Lord;
  may your love and your truth always protect me.

PSALM 40:11

The Lord is faithful, and he will strengthen and protect you from the evil one.

2 THESSALONIANS 3:3

Discretion will protect you,
  and understanding will guard you.

PROVERBS 2:11

God's Words of Life on

PROTECTION

"Because he loves me," says the LORD, "I will rescue him;
I will protect him, for he acknowledges my name.
He will call upon me, and I will answer him;
I will be with him in trouble,
I will deliver him and honor him.
With long life will I satisfy him
and show him my salvation."

PSALM 91:14-16

You are my hiding place, LORD;
you will protect me from trouble
and surround me with songs of deliverance.

PSALM 32:7

Show the wonder of your great love, LORD,
you who save by your right hand
those who take refuge in you from their foes.
Keep me as the apple of your eye;
hide me in the shadow of your wings.

PSALM 17:7-8

PROTECTION

Because you are my help,
I sing in the shadow of your wings, O God.
My soul clings to you;
your right hand upholds me.

PSALM 63:7-8

My help comes from the LORD,
the Maker of heaven and earth.
He will not let your foot slip—
he who watches over you will not slumber;
indeed, he who watches over Israel
will neither slumber nor sleep.
The LORD watches over you—
the LORD is your shade at your right hand;
the sun will not harm you by day,
nor the moon by night.
The LORD will keep you from all harm—
he will watch over your life;
the LORD will watch over your coming and going
both now and forevermore.

PSALM 121:2-8

God's Words of Life on

PROTECTION

He who dwells in the shelter of the Most High
    will rest in the shadow of the Almighty.
I will say of the LORD, "He is my refuge and my
fortress,
    my God, in whom I trust." ...
He will cover you with his feathers,
    and under his wings you will find refuge;
    his faithfulness will be your shield and rampart.
You will not fear the terror of night,
    nor the arrow that flies by day,
nor the pestilence that stalks in the darkness,
    nor the plague that destroys at midday.
A thousand may fall at your side,
    ten thousand at your right hand,
    but it will not come near you. ...
If you make the Most High your dwelling—
    even the LORD, who is my refuge—
then no harm will befall you,
    no disaster will come near your tent.
For he will command his angels concerning you
    to guard you in all your ways.

PSALM 91:1-2, 4-7, 9-11

GOD'S ARMOR

In Ephesians 6:10-18 we read that God has provided weapons for our use and protection. He has given us a full suit of armor to protect us from evil:

- **The Belt of Truth**—your defense against the lies of the enemy. God's Word is a filter to differentiate between truth and lies (Ephesians 1:13).

- **The Breastplate of Righteousness**—your protection against the enemy's accusations. Jesus took your sin on himself, and you are now righteous in God's eyes (2 Corinthians 5:21).

- **The Shoes of the Gospel of Peace**—your defense against retreat. Your peace comes in knowing that you have all you need in Christ (Philippians 4:19).

- **The Shield of Faith**—your defense against doubt and guilt (Hebrews 10:22).

- 🍀 **The Helmet of Salvation**—your defense against confusion and wrong thinking (Romans 12:2, 2 Corinthians 10:5). They rob you of your assurance of salvation.

- 🍀 **The Sword of the Spirit**—the *rhema* ("spoken") Word of God. When God says it and you speak it out, the Spirit cuts through the darkness like a sword (Hebrews 4:12).

As you grow and mature in Christ, the protctive wall of faith guarding your heart grows taller, thicker, and more impervious to attack. Put on—or "pray on"—God's armor every morning. God will protect you and bring you joy, even in the battle, because he is your strength and song (Exodus 15:2).

God's Words of Life on

REST

Jesus said, "Come to me, all you who are weary and burdened, and I will give you rest. Take my yoke upon you and learn from me, for I am gentle and humble in heart, and you will find rest for your souls. For my yoke is easy and my burden is light."

MATTHEW 11:28-30

I will lie down and sleep in peace,
    for you alone, O LORD,
    make me dwell in safety.

PSALM 4:8

The LORD is gracious and righteous;
    our God is full of compassion.
The LORD protects the simplehearted;
    when I was in great need, he saved me.
Be at rest once more, O my soul,
    for the LORD has been good to you.

PSALM 116:5-7

God's Words of Life on

REST

I have set the LORD always before me.
    Because he is at my right hand,
    I will not be shaken.
Therefore my heart is glad and my tongue rejoices;
    my body also will rest secure.

PSALM 16:8-9

When you lie down, you will not be afraid;
    When you lie down, your sleep will be sweet.

PROVERBS 3:24

Ask where the good way is, and walk in it,
    and you will find rest for your souls.

JEREMIAH 6:16

My soul finds rest in God alone;
    my salvation comes from him.

PSALM 62:1

God's Words of Life on

REST

By the seventh day [of creation] God had finished
the work he had been doing; so on the seventh day
he rested from all his work. And God blessed the
seventh day and made it holy, because on it he rested
from all the work of creating that he had done.

GENESIS 2:2-3

In repentance and rest is your salvation,
    in quietness and trust is your strength.

ISAIAH 30:15

Then, because so many people were coming and
going that they did not even have a chance to eat,
Jesus said to [his disciples], "Come with me by yourselves to a quiet place and get some rest."

MARK 6:31

He who dwells in the shelter of the Most High
    will rest in the shadow of the Almighty.

PSALM 91:1

God's Words of Life on

REST

Find rest, O my soul, in God alone;
my hope comes from him.

PSALM 62:5

"My people will live in peaceful dwelling places,
in secure homes,
in undisturbed places of rest," says the LORD.

ISAIAH 32:18

There remains, then, a Sabbath-rest for the people of
God; for anyone who enters God's rest also rests
from his own work, just as God did from his.

HEBREWS 4:9-10

The fear of the LORD leads to life:
Then one rests content, untouched by trouble.

PROVERBS 19:23

I lie down and sleep; I wake again,
because the LORD sustains me.

PSALM 3:5

God's Words of Life on

REST

God grants sleep to those he loves.

PSALM 127:2

My heart is not proud, O LORD,
    my eyes are not haughty;
I do not concern myself with great matters
    or things too wonderful for me.
But I have stilled and quieted my soul;
    like a weaned child with its mother,
    like a weaned child is my soul within me.

PSALM 131:1-2

You gave abundant showers, O God;
    you refreshed your weary inheritance.

PSALM 68:9

"I will refresh the weary and satisfy the faint," says
the LORD.

JEREMIAH 31:25

Devotional Thought on Rest
REST IN THE LORD

"Busy" is becoming the universal response to "How are you?" in today's fast-paced world. People seem to rate their worth and recognition on the relentless busyness of their schedules. Who has time for a contemplative thought when every moment is filled with activity? And who would ever consider the idea of rest?

In Matthew 11:28-30 Jesus says, "Come to me, all you who are weary and burdened, and I will give you rest. Take my yoke upon you and learn from me, for I am gentle and humble in heart, and you will find rest for your souls. For my yoke is easy and my burden is light." A yoke is a wooden frame placed across the necks of two animals (often oxen), so they can work together. A young, inexperienced ox is oftened trained in a yoke with an experienced, older ox. If the younger ox tries to run ahead or pull away, it gets a stiff neck, but it is still connected to the older, steady ox. Eventually the younger one will learn from the older one.

Jesus wants you to voluntarily take his yoke and learn from him. His gentleness will continually guide you in the right direction. In him you will find rest for your weary soul.

God's Words of Life on

SALVATION

"God so loved the world that he gave his one and only Son, that whoever believes in him shall not perish but have eternal life. For God did not send his Son into the world to condemn the world, but to save the world through him."

JOHN 3:16-17

The LORD is my rock, my fortress and my deliverer;
    my God is my rock, in whom I take refuge.
He is my shield and the horn of my salvation,
    my stronghold.

PSALM 18:2

Jesus said, "The Son of Man came to seek and to save what was lost."

LUKE 19:10

Jesus said, "My Father's will is that everyone who looks to the Son and believes in him shall have eternal life, and I will raise him up at the last day."

JOHN 6:40

God's Words of Life on

SALVATION

I know that the LORD saves his anointed;
he answers him from his holy heaven
with the saving power of his right hand.
Some trust in chariots and some in horses,
but we trust in the name of the LORD our God.

PSALM 20:6-7

Christ was sacrificed once to take away the sins of
many people; and he will appear a second time, not
to bear sin, but to bring salvation to those who are
waiting for him.

HEBREWS 9:28

The LORD is the strength of his people,
a fortress of salvation for his anointed one.
Save your people and bless your inheritance;
be their shepherd and carry them forever.

PSALM 28:8-9

Jesus is able to save completely those who come to
God through him, because he always lives to inter-
cede for them.

HEBREWS 7:25

God's Words of Life on

SALVATION

The grace of God that brings salvation has appeared to all men. It teaches us to say "No" to ungodliness and worldly passions, and to live self-controlled, upright and godly lives in this present age, while we wait for the blessed hope—the glorious appearing of our great God and Savior, Jesus Christ, who gave himself for us to redeem us from all wickedness and to purify for himself a people that are his very own, eager to do what is good.

TITUS 2:11-14

The salvation of the righteous comes from the LORD;
*   he is their stronghold in time of trouble.*

PSALM 37:39

If you confess with your mouth, "Jesus is Lord," and believe in your heart that God raised him from the dead, you will be saved.

ROMANS 10:9

The LORD takes delight in his people;
*   he crowns the humble with salvation.*

PSALM 149:4

SALVATION

The LORD is my strength and my song;
*   he has become my salvation.*

PSALM 118:14

Jesus said, "Whoever drinks the water I give him
will never thirst. Indeed, the water I give him will
become in him a spring of water welling up to eter-
nal life."

JOHN 4:14

In him we were also chosen, having been predes-
tined according to the plan of him who works out
everything in conformity with the purpose of his
will, in order that we, who were the first to hope in
Christ, might be for the praise of his glory. And you
also were included in Christ when you heard the
word of truth, the gospel of your salvation. Having
believed, you were marked in him with a seal, the
promised Holy Spirit, who is a deposit guaranteeing
our inheritance until the redemption of those who
are God's possession—to the praise of his glory.

EPHESIANS 1:11-14

God's Words of Life on

SALVATION

Jesus said, *"My sheep listen to my voice; I know them, and they follow me. I give them eternal life, and they shall never perish; no one can snatch them out of my hand."*

JOHN 10:27-28

Because of his great love for us, God, who is rich in mercy, made us alive with Christ even when we were dead in transgressions—it is by grace you have been saved. And God raised us up with Christ and seated us with him in the heavenly realms in Christ Jesus, in order that in the coming ages he might show the incomparable riches of his grace, expressed in his kindness to us in Christ Jesus. For it is by grace you have been saved, through faith—and this not from yourselves, it is the gift of God—not by works, so that no one can boast.

EPHESIANS 2:4-9

I will give you thanks, for you answered me, O LORD; you have become my salvation.

PSALM 118:21

SALVATION

Jesus said, "I tell you the truth, whoever hears my word and believes him who sent me has eternal life and will not be condemned; he has crossed over from death to life."

JOHN 5:24

Jesus prayed, "Now this is eternal life: that they may know you, the only true God, and Jesus Christ, whom you have sent."

JOHN 17:3

The wages of sin is death, but the gift of God is eternal life in Christ Jesus our Lord.

ROMANS 6:23

Jesus said, "I am the resurrection and the life. He who believes in me will live, even though he dies; and whoever lives and believes in me will never die."

JOHN 11:25-26

God's Words of Life on

SALVATION

The LORD is my light and my salvation—
whom shall I fear?
The LORD is the stronghold of my life—
of whom shall I be afraid?

PSALM 27:1

Jesus said, "I tell you the truth, he who believes has
everlasting life. I am the bread of life. ... Here is the
bread that comes down from heaven, which a man
may eat and not die. I am the living bread that came
down from heaven. If anyone eats of this bread, he
will live forever. This bread is my flesh, which I will
give for the life of the world."

JOHN 6:47-48, 50-51

The LORD redeems his servants;
no one will be condemned
who takes refuge in him.

PSALM 34:22

THE TORN CURTAIN

The ark of the covenant is the curtain separating the Holy Place from the Most Holy Place and the Most Holy Place itself, where God meets with Moses.

The curtain separating the Holy Place from the Most Holy Place shields the ark (the symbol of God's presence) from view. This shield not only keeps the priests from seeing God's glory, but also prevents God's glory from being in the presence of sin, which would mean certain death for those in the tabernacle. At Christ's death, this curtain was wondrously torn in two from top to bottom (Matthew 27:51). All believers today, not just the high priest, have access to the Most Holy Place because of the shed blood of Jesus (Hebrews 10:19-20).

God has cleared the way for you to enter his presence through his Son's death and resurrection. Picture Jesus standing between the Holy Place and the Most Holy Place with his arms outstretched. If you desire to go into the presence of God, you must walk into his arms and accept his love. Nothing else will matter. You will be complete in him, enjoying his presence, his love, and his salvation.

SHARING THE GOOD NEWS

Jesus said, "Go and make disciples of all nations, baptizing them in the name of the Father and of the Son and of the Holy Spirit, and teaching them to obey everything I have commanded you. And surely I am with you always, to the very end of the age."

MATTHEW 28:19-20

I urge ... that requests, prayers, intercession and thanksgiving be made for everyone—for kings and all those in authority, that we may live peaceful and quiet lives in all godliness and holiness. This is good, and pleases God our Savior, who wants all men to be saved and to come to a knowledge of the truth.

1 TIMOTHY 2:1-4

Thanks be to God, who always leads us in triumphal procession in Christ and through us spreads every-where the fragrance of the knowledge of him. For we are to God the aroma of Christ among those who are being saved and those who are perishing.

2 CORINTHIANS 2:14-15

SHARING THE GOOD NEWS

All over the world this gospel is bearing fruit and growing.

COLOSSIANS 1:6

I do not hide your righteousness in my heart, O LORD;
*   I speak of your faithfulness and salvation.*
I do not conceal your love and your truth
*   from the great assembly.*

PSALM 40:10

If one of you should wander from the truth and some-
one should bring him back, remember this: Whoever
turns a sinner from the error of his way will save him
from death and cover over a multitude of sins.

JAMES 5:19-20

God, who said, "Let light shine out of darkness,"
made his light shine in our hearts to give us the light
of the knowledge of the glory of God in the face of
Christ. But we have this treasure in jars of clay to
show that this all-surpassing power is from God and
not from us.

2 CORINTHIANS 4:6-7

God's Words of Life on

SHARING THE GOOD NEWS

I will declare your name to my brothers, LORD;
    in the congregation I will praise you.

PSALM 22:22

Though I am free and belong to no man, I make
myself a slave to everyone, to win as many as possi-
ble. ... I have become all things to all men so that by
all possible means I might save some. I do all this for
the sake of the gospel, that I may share in its bless-
ings.

1 CORINTHIANS 9:19, 22-23

My mouth will tell of your righteousness,
    of your salvation all day long,
        though I know not its measure.
I will come and proclaim your mighty acts,
        O Sovereign LORD;
    I will proclaim your righteousness, yours alone.

PSALM 71:15-16

God's Words of Life on

SHARING THE GOOD NEWS

God did not give us a spirit of timidity, but a spirit of power, of love and of self-discipline. So do not be ashamed to testify about our Lord.

2 TIMOTHY 1:7-8

How beautiful on the mountains
*   are the feet of those who bring good news,*
who proclaim peace,
*   who bring good tidings,*
*   who proclaim salvation,*
who say to Zion,
*   "Your God reigns!"*

ISAIAH 52:7

I try to please everybody in every way. For I am not seeking my own good but the good of many, so that they may be saved.

1 CORINTHIANS 10:33

I am not ashamed of the gospel, because it is the power of God for the salvation of everyone who believes.

ROMANS 1:16

God's Words of Life on

SHARING THE GOOD NEWS

Jesus said, "Whoever wants to save his life will lose it, but whoever loses his life for me and for the gospel will save it."

MARK 8:35

This is the testimony: God has given us eternal life, and this life is in his Son.

1 JOHN 5:11

We know that we live in God and he in us, because he has given us of his Spirit. And we have seen and testify that the Father has sent his Son to be the Savior of the world. If anyone acknowledges that Jesus is the Son of God, God lives in him and he in God.

1 JOHN 4:13-15

Jesus said, "You will receive power when the Holy Spirit comes on you; and you will be my witnesses in Jerusalem, and in all Judea and Samaria, and to the ends of the earth."

ACTS 1:8

Devotional Thought on Sharing the Good News
A GOD-ORDAINED MEETING

The story of Philip and the Ethiopian eunuch teaches that meeting people where they are and allowing God to work is the best approach when sharing your faith. Philip was given a simple command: "Go south to the road" (Acts 8:26). There Philip comes across the Ethiopian man, reading the book of Isaiah. Philip simply asks him if he understands what he is reading. The eunuch's response is: "How can I understand this stuff unless someone explains it to me?" Philip doesn't have to push his beliefs on the man. The man *invites* Philip to explain the Scriptures to him. Are there people in your life who want you to explain the Good News to them? Who are they? What will you do?

Philip explains the Good News by beginning with the very passage the eunuch is reading. Philip meets the eunuch where he is, and he proceeds from that point.

Make a list of your family members, friends, and acquaintances who need to hear the gospel. Ask God to give you sensitivity to his Spirit during times of contact with these people. In the coming days and weeks, pray for each person on your list and ask God to make a "divine appointment" with her or with him.

God's Words of Life on

STRENGTH

Those who hope in the LORD
will renew their strength.
They will soar on wings like eagles;
they will run and not grow weary,
they will walk and not be faint.

ISAIAH 40:31

Jesus said, "My grace is sufficient for you, for my
power is made perfect in weakness." Therefore I will
boast all the more gladly about my weaknesses, so
that Christ's power may rest on me.

2 CORINTHIANS 12:9

The LORD is my strength and my shield;
my heart trusts in him, and I am helped.
My heart leaps for joy
and I will give thanks to him in song.

PSALM 28:7

The joy of the LORD is your strength.

NEHEMIAH 8:10

STRENGTH

God is our refuge and strength,
an ever-present help in trouble.
Therefore we will not fear, though the earth give way
and the mountains fall into the heart of the sea,
though its waters roar and foam
and the mountains quake with their surging.

PSALM 46:1-3

I can do everything through Christ who gives me
strength.

PHILIPPIANS 4:13

Surely God is my salvation;
I will trust and not be afraid
The LORD, the LORD, is my strength and my song;
he has become my salvation.

ISAIAH 12:2

The Lord stood at my side and gave me strength, so that
through me the message might be fully proclaimed.

2 TIMOTHY 4:17

God's Words of Life on

STRENGTH

"*Do not fear, for I am with you;*
do not be dismayed, for I am your God.
I will strengthen you and help you;
I will uphold you with my righteous right hand."

ISAIAH 41:10

Be strong in the Lord and in his mighty power.

EPHESIANS 6:10

The LORD *gives strength to his people;*
the LORD *blesses his people with peace.*

PSALM 29:11

I pray ... that you may know ... God's incomparably
great power for us who believe. That power is like
the working of his mighty strength, which he exerted
in Christ when he raised him from the dead and
seated him at his right hand in the heavenly realms.

EPHESIANS 1:18-20

God's Words of Life on

STRENGTH

Nothing is impossible with God.

LUKE 1:37

*The LORD gives strength to the weary
    and increases the power of the weak.*

ISAIAH 40:29

*The Sovereign LORD is my strength;
    he makes my feet like the feet of a deer,
    he enables me to go on the heights.*

HABAKKUK 3:19

*One thing God has spoken,
    two things have I heard:
    that you, O God, are strong,
    and that you, O LORD, are loving.*

PSALM 62:11-12

*O my Strength, I watch for you;
    you, O God, are my fortress, my loving God.*

PSALM 59:9-10

God's Words of Life on
STRENGTH

From the ends of the earth I call to you, LORD,
 I call as my heart grows faint;
 lead me to the rock that is higher than I.
For you have been my refuge,
 a strong tower against the foe.

PSALM 61:2-3

*The God of all grace, who called you to his eternal
glory in Christ, after you have suffered a little while,
will himself restore you and make you strong, firm
and steadfast.*

1 PETER 5:10

Glory in his holy name;
 *let the hearts of those who seek the LORD
rejoice.*
Look to the LORD and his strength;
 seek his face always.

PSALM 105:3-4

The name of the LORD is a strong tower;
 the righteous run to it and are safe.

PROVERBS 18:10

Devotional Thought on Strength
WARRIOR WOMAN

Deborah is a woman among men—brave, intelligent, trustworthy, sure of God's words and confident of God's presence. Deborah rules Israel under a palm tree that bears her name. The Israelites bring all their disputes to her. But more than an arbitrator, Deborah is a conduit of God's will for the people.

Deborah steps outside of that day's common cultural position for women. She judges while most women are at home weaving. She prophesies when her peers are cooking meals. And she goes into battle while other women stay at home with the children.

The key issue here, however, is not what Deborah does but whom she follows. Deborah willingly does whatever God asks of her. She would have been just as willing to stay at home with the kids. But God calls her into battle. Deborah doesn't quibble or quake. She obeys, and receives incredible strength from God. You, too, can receive God's strength for the battles of your life through faithful obedience to the Lord.

God's Words of Life on

TRUST

When I am afraid,
      I will trust in you.
In God, whose word I praise,
      in God I trust; I will not be afraid.
      What can mortal man do to me?

PSALM 56:3-4

Trust in the LORD with all you heart
      and lean not on your own understanding;
in all your ways acknowledge him,
      and he will make your paths straight.

PROVERBS 3:5-6

Let him who walks in the dark,
      who has no light,
trust in the name of the LORD
      and rely on his God.

ISAIAH 50:10

Those who know your name will trust in you,
      for you, LORD, have never forsaken those who
      seek you.

PSALM 9:10

God's Words of Life on

TRUST

The LORD is good,
    a refuge in times of trouble.
He cares for those who trust in him.

NAHUM 1:7

Let the morning bring me word of your unfailing love,
    for I have put my trust in you.
Show me the way I should go,
    for to you I lift up my soul.

PSALM 143:8

Commit your way to the LORD;
    trust in him and he will do this:
He will make your righteousness shine like the dawn,
    the justice of your cause like the noonday sun.

PSALM 37:5-6

Those who trust in the LORD are like Mount Zion,
    which cannot be shaken but endures forever.

PSALM 125:1

God's Words of Life on

TRUST

You will keep in perfect peace, LORD,
him whose mind is steadfast,
because he trusts in you.

ISAIAH 26:3

I am still confident of this:
I will see the goodness of the LORD
in the land of the living.
Wait for the LORD;
be strong and take heart
and wait for the LORD.

PSALM 27:13-14

Trust in the LORD forever,
for the LORD, the LORD, is the Rock eternal.

ISAIAH 26:4

God's Words of Life on

TRUST

Surely this is our God;
     we trusted in him, and he saved us.
This is the LORD, we trusted in him;
     let us rejoice and be glad in his salvation.

ISAIAH 25:9

So this is what the Sovereign LORD says:
"See, I lay a stone in Zion,
     a tested stone,
a precious cornerstone for a sure foundation;
     the one who trusts will never be dismayed."

ISAIAH 28:16

Jesus said, *"Do not let your hearts be troubled. Trust in God; trust also in me."*

JOHN 14:1

In repentance and rest is your salvation,
     in quietness and trust is your strength.

ISAIAH 30:15

God's Words of Life on

TRUST

Blessed is the man who trusts in the LORD,
    whose confidence is in him.
He will be like a tree planted by the water
    that sends out its roots by the stream.
It does not fear when heat comes;
    its leaves are always green.
It has no worries in a year of drought
    and never fails to bear fruit.

JEREMIAH 17:7-8

Anyone who trusts in Jesus will never be put to shame.

ROMANS 10:11

May the God of hope fill you with all joy and peace as you trust in him, so that you may overflow with hope by the power of the Holy Spirit.

ROMANS 15:13

TRUSTING WHEN TESTED

The prophet Habakkuk lived in a time of distress and desperation. Wickedness and oppression surround him. In frustration Habakkuk asked God, "Where are you in all this?" God then reveals his plan to punish the rebellion and wickedness of his people. Despite Habakkuk's circumstances and the coming calamity God has shown him, he chooses to rejoice.

When you are in the midst of a distressing situation do you, like Habakkuk, wonder, *Where are you, God?* Perhaps your faith is being tested and you need to learn what Habakkuk comes to understand.

When you face trials and testing, you have a choice. You can choose to trust the strength of the Lord, as Habakkuk does, or you can choose to rely on yourself. Depending on yourself results in corruption and deception. Depending on God results in the ability to rejoice regardless of circumstances.

If you are enduring testing, be aware of the clear choices before you. If you trust in worldly power or your own understanding, you will be disappointed. But "the LORD is good, a refuge in times of trouble." (Nahum 1:7). Trust him, and be filled with joy, peace and hope (Romans 15:13).

God's Words of Life on

WISDOM

The fear of the LORD is the beginning of wisdom,
and knowledge of the Holy One is understanding.

PROVERBS 9:10

The wisdom that comes from heaven is first of all
pure; then peace-loving, considerate, submissive, full
of mercy and good fruit, impartial and sincere.

JAMES 3:17

He who walks with the wise grows wise.

PROVERBS 13:20

Know also that wisdom is sweet to your soul;
if you find it, there is a future hope for you,
and your hope will not be cut off.

PROVERBS 24:14

If any of you lacks wisdom, he should ask God, who
gives generously to all without finding fault, and it
will be given to him.

JAMES 1:5

God's Words of Life on

WISDOM

Praise be to the name of God for ever and ever;
wisdom and power are his.
He changes times and seasons;
he sets up kings and deposes them.
He gives wisdom to the wise
and knowledge to the discerning.

DANIEL 2:20-21

I keep asking that the God of our Lord Jesus Christ,
the glorious Father, may give you the Spirit of wisdom and revelation, so that you may know him better.

EPHESIANS 1:17

Get wisdom, get understanding;
do not forget my words or swerve from them.
Do not forsake wisdom, and she will protect you;
love her, and she will watch over you.
Wisdom is supreme, therefore get wisdom.
Though it cost all you have, get understanding.

PROVERBS 4:5-7

God's Words of Life on

WISDOM

*Teach us to number our days aright, O LORD,
    that we may gain a heart of wisdom.*

PSALM 90:12

*Surely you desire truth in the inner parts, LORD;
    you teach me wisdom in the inmost place.*

PSALM 51:6

*Wisdom, like an inheritance, is a good thing
    and benefits those who see the sun.
Wisdom is a shelter
    as money is a shelter,
but the advantage of knowledge is this:
    that wisdom preserves the life of its possessor.*

ECCLESIASTES 7:11-12

*He who gets wisdom loves his own soul;
    he who cherishes understanding prospers.*

PROVERBS 19:8

WISDOM

A wife of noble character who can find?
She ... works with eager hands. ...
She gets up while it is still dark;
>   *she provides food for her family. ...*
She sets about her work vigorously;
>   *her arms are strong for her tasks. ...*
She opens her arms to the poor
>   *and extends her hands to the needy.*
When it snows, she has no fear for her household;
>   *for all of them are clothed in scarlet. ...*
She is clothed with strength and dignity;
>   *she can laugh at the days to come.*
She speaks with wisdom,
>   *and faithful instruction is on her tongue. ...*
Her children arise and call her blessed;
>   *her husband also, and he praises her:*
"Many women do noble things,
>   *but you surpass them all."*
Charm is deceptive, and beauty is fleeting;
>   *but a woman who fears the LORD is to be*
praised.

PROVERBS 31:10, 13, 15, 17, 20-21, 25-26, 28-30

God's Words of Life on

WISDOM

*If you call out for insight
    and cry aloud for understanding,
and if you look for it as for silver
    and search for it as for hidden treasure,
then you will understand the fear of the LORD
    and find the knowledge of God.*

PROVERBS 2:3-5

*Those who are wise will shine like the brightness of
the heavens, and those who lead many to righteousness, like the stars for ever and ever.*

DANIEL 12:3

*The fear of the LORD is the beginning of wisdom;
    all who follow his precepts
have good understanding.
    To him belongs eternal praise.*

PSALM 111:10

Devotional Thought on Wisdom

CONSTRUCTION AND INTERIOR DESIGN

Imagine you are planning to build a new home. First you go to a good architect—one you trust to draw up a good plan. Next you find qualified builders to do the construction and artisans to finish the work. After the building is completed, you furnish it with your personal treasures to make your house a home.

Each day you are in the process of building a spiritual house. What determines your plans and influences your decisions? Is your life built on a solid foundation? It's never too late to do some remodeling.

Plan and build your house by wisdom. Its value is beyond comprehension. Make wisdom the basis for all that is planned, built and done in your life. Do you feel incapable of building anything of value? You can ask the master builder and architect of the universe to help you. He has given you Jesus Christ, "in whom are hidden all the treasures of wisdom and knowledge" (Colossians 2:3).

God's Words of Life on

WORK

*May the favor of the LORD our God rest upon us;
    establish the work of our hands for us—
    yes, establish the work of our hands.*

PSALM 90:17

*Whatever you do, work at it with all your heart, as
working for the Lord, not for men, since you know
that you will receive an inheritance from the Lord as
a reward. It is the Lord Christ you are serving.*

COLOSSIANS 3:23-24

*The man who plants and the man who waters have
one purpose, and each will be rewarded according to
his own labor. For we are God's fellow workers; you
are God's field, God's building.*

1 CORINTHIANS 3:8-9

*God is not unjust; he will not forget your work and
the love you have shown him as you have helped his
people and continue to help them.*

HEBREWS 6:10

God's Words of Life on

WORK

We are God's workmanship, created in Christ Jesus
to do good works, which God prepared in advance
for us to do.

EPHESIANS 2:10

Whatever you do, whether in word or deed, do it all
in the name of the Lord Jesus, giving thanks to God
the Father through him.

COLOSSIANS 3:17

All hard work brings a profit.

PROVERBS 14:23

Six days you shall labor and do all your work, but
the seventh day is a Sabbath to the LORD your God.
On it you shall not do any work.

DEUTERONOMY 5:13-14

Serve wholeheartedly, as if you were serving the
Lord, not men, because you know that the Lord will
reward everyone for whatever good he does.

EPHESIANS 6:7-8

God's Words of Life on

WORK

My heart took delight in all my work,
and this was the reward for all my labor.

ECCLESIASTES 2:10

Blessed are all who fear the LORD,
who walk in his ways.
You will eat the fruit of your labor;
blessings and prosperity will be yours.

PSALM 128:1-2

By hard work we must help the weak, remembering
the words the Lord Jesus himself said: "It is more
blessed to give than to receive."

ACTS 20:35

The plans of the diligent lead to profit.

PROVERBS 21:5

The LORD your God has blessed you in all the work
of your hands.

DEUTERONOMY 2:7

THE POSSIBILITIES ARE ENDLESS

If we read the detailed description of the ideal wife and mother in Proverbs 31 as the point-by-point standard God expects us to live up to, we're bound to feel overwhelmed and exhausted before we even begin! The intention of this epilogue to the book of Proverbs wasn't to give women an impossible to-do list, but to spread out before them the many opportunities they have to use their gifts, talents, and wisdom in fulfilling and productive ways. Rather than limiting women's roles, they are expanded endlessly.

As women we are created to have a positive and profound impact on everyone around us—whether it be our husbands, children, parents, friends, clients, customers, or society in general. Being a woman is a blessing, and being a wise, strong and dignified woman blesses others in way that can't be calculated, whatever the work we choose to do.

WORRY

Jesus said, "Do not worry about your life, what you will eat or drink; or about your body, what you will wear. Is not life more important than food, and the body more important than clothes? Look at the birds of the air; they do not sow or reap or store away in barns, and yet your heavenly Father feeds them. Are you not much more valuable than they?"

MATTHEW 6:25-26

Why are you downcast, O my soul?
 Why so disturbed within me?
Put your hope in God,
 for I will yet praise him,
 my Savior and my God.

PSALM 42:11

Cast your cares on the LORD
 and he will sustain you;
 he will never let the righteous fall.

PSALM 55:22

God's Words of Life on

WORRY

Trust in the LORD and do good;
dwell in the land and enjoy safe pasture.
Delight yourself in the LORD
and he will give you the desires of your heart.

PSALM 37:3-4

Do not be anxious about anything, but in every-
thing, by prayer and petition, with thanksgiving,
present your requests to God. And the peace of God,
which transcends all understanding, will guard your
hearts and your minds in Christ Jesus.

PHILIPPIANS 4:6-7

Cast all your anxiety on God because he cares for
you.

1 PETER 5:7

If the LORD delights in a man's way,
he makes his steps firm;
though he stumble, he will not fall,
for the LORD upholds him with his hand.

PSALM 37:23-24

WORRY

God is just: He will pay back trouble to those who trouble you and give relief to you who are troubled, and to us as well. This will happen when the Lord Jesus is revealed from heaven in blazing fire with his powerful angels.

2 THESSALONIANS 1:6-7

The LORD is faithful to all his promises
    and loving toward all he has made.
The LORD upholds all those who fall
    and lifts up all who are bowed down.

PSALM 145:13-14

Surely God is my help;
    the LORD is the one who sustains me.

PSALM 54:4

God's Words of Life on

WORRY

Let all who take refuge in you be glad;
let them ever sing for joy.
Spread your protection over them,
that those who love your name may rejoice in
you.
For surely, O LORD, you bless the righteous;
you surround them with your favor as
with a shield.

PSALM 5:11-12

Praise be to the LORD, to God our Savior,
who daily bears our burdens.

PSALM 68:19

"When you pass through the waters,
I will be with you;
and when you pass through the rivers,
they will not sweep over you.
When you walk through the fire,
you will not be burned;
the flames will not set you ablaze," says the LORD.

ISAIAH 43:2

God's Words of Life on

WORRY

Jesus said, "Why do you worry about clothes? See how the lilies of the field grow. They do not labor or spin. Yet I tell you that not even Solomon in all his splendor was dressed like one of these. If that is how God clothes the grass of the field, which is here today and tomorrow is thrown into the fire, will he not much more clothe you? ... So do not worry, saying, 'What shall we eat?' or 'What shall we drink?' or 'What shall we wear?' For ... your heavenly Father knows that you need them. But seek first his kingdom and his righteousness, and all these things will be given to you as well. Therefore do not worry about tomorrow, for tomorrow will worry about itself. Each day has enough trouble of its own."

MATTHEW 6:28-34

LETTING GO

In Psalm 55:16-17 David brings his concerns and fears to God, asking him to take over and take care of the problems he's facing: *"I call to God, and the LORD saves me. Evening, morning, and noon I cry out in distress and he hears my voice."* He knows he can trust God with the outcome. God has proven himself before and will do so again.

Most of the time, what we worry about is not entirely within our control. We can't dictate the results of our best efforts; we can't force our hopes to materialize; and we definitely can't make someone we love healthy and happy by the sheer force of our will. When we try to control outcomes, we carry a burden too heavy for human shoulders to bear.

What a relief it is to finally let go, to heave our heavy burden onto the strong back of the Lord. He promises to sustain our hearts and minds with his peace (Philippians 4:6-7). And no matter what he chooses to do with what concerns us, we have the assurance that his decisions are guided by his love for us.

God's Words of Life on

WORSHIP

Jesus said, "A time is coming and has now come
when the true worshipers will worship the Father in
spirit and truth, for they are the kind of worshipers
the Father seeks."

JOHN 4:23

Worship the LORD with gladness;
    come before him with joyful songs. ...
Enter his gates with thanksgiving
    and his courts with praise;
    give thanks to him and praise his name.
For the LORD is good and his love endures forever;
    his faithfulness continues through all generations.

PSALM 100:2, 4-5

Come, let us bow down in worship,
    let us kneel before the LORD our Maker;
for he is our God
    and we are the people of his pasture,
    the flock under his care.

PSALM 95:6-7

God's Words of Life on

WORSHIP

Since we are receiving a kingdom that cannot be shaken, let us be thankful, and so worship God acceptably with reverence and awe.

HEBREWS 12:28

I will praise you, O LORD my God, with all my heart;
*   I will glorify your name forever.*
For great is your love toward me.

PSALM 86:12-13

Let the heavens rejoice, let the earth be glad;
*   let them say among the nations, "The LORD reigns!"*
Let the sea resound, and all that is in it;
*   let the fields be jubilant, and everything in them!*
Then the trees of the forest will sing,
*   they will sing for joy before the LORD,*
*   for he comes to judge the earth.*
Give thanks to the LORD, for he is good;
*   his love endures forever.*

1 CHRONICLES 16:31-34

God's Words of Life on

WORSHIP

Stand up and praise the LORD your God, who is from everlasting to everlasting. Blessed be your glorious name, and may it be exalted above all blessing and praise. You alone are the LORD. You made the heavens, even the highest heavens, and all their starry host, the earth and all that is on it, the seas and all that is in them. You give life to everything, and the multitudes of heaven worship you.

NEHEMIAH 9:5-6

In the day of my trouble I will call to you,
*   for you will answer me.*
Among the gods there is none like you, O LORD;
*   no deeds can compare with yours.*
All the nations you have made
*   will come and worship before you, O LORD;*
*   they will bring glory to your name.*
For you are great and do marvelous deeds;
*   you alone are God.*

PSALM 86:7-10

WORSHIP

I have seen you in the sanctuary
and beheld your power and your glory.
Because your love is better than life,
my lips will glorify you.

PSALM 63:2-4

Ascribe to the LORD, O families of nations,
Ascribe to the LORD glory and strength,
Ascribe to the LORD the glory due his name.
Bring an offering and come before him;
Worship the LORD in the splendor of his holiness.

1 CHRONICLES 16:28-29

All the angels were standing around the throne and
around the elders and the four living creatures. They
fell down on their faces before the throne and wor-
shiped God, saying: "Amen! Praise and glory and
wisdom and thanks and honor and power and
strength be to our God for ever and ever. Amen!"

REVELATION 7:11-12

God's Words of Life on

WORSHIP

Jesus said, "A time is coming and has now come when the true worshipers will worship the Father in spirit and truth, for they are the kind of worshipers the Father seeks. God is spirit, and his worshipers must worship in spirit and in truth."

JOHN 4:23-24

...Those who had been victorious...held harps given them by God and sang the song of Moses the servant of God and the song of the Lamb: "Great and marvelous are your deeds, Lord God Almighty. Just and true are your ways, King of the ages. Who will not fear you, O Lord, and bring glory to your name? For you alone are holy. All nations will come and worship before you, for your righteous acts have been revealed."

REVELATION 15:2-4

Praise the LORD. How good it is to sing praises to our God,

how pleasant and fitting to praise him!

PSALM 147:1

EXTRAVAGANT WORSHIP

In Luke 7:36-50 we read of a "sinful" woman who endures ridicule when she comes into the house of a Pharisee and approaches Jesus. Her tears wet his feet; she wipes his feet with her hair and kisses them. Then she pours her perfume over them. What a beautiful act of worship! But those around her respond with indignation and offense. Her expression of worship is completely misunderstood by everyone except Jesus.

Imagine you are this woman. Are you embarrassed? Or are you focusing so intently on Jesus that you neither notice nor care about the reactions of others? Worship is a time of intimacy between you and your Lord. Don't let a desire for the approval of others prevent you from offering loving abandonment to God.

Offering a "sacrifice of praise" (Hebrews 13:15) to the Lord requires that you sacrifice your own ideas and those of others in order to hold God's honor as supreme. Whatever your style, whatever your circumstance, whatever your condition— praise him!

Other titles to enjoy in the
God's Words of Life Series include:

God's Words of Life for Young Women of Faith from
the *Young Women of Faith Study Bible NIV*

God's Words of Life for Moms from the
New International Version

More of God's Words of Life for Women from the
New International Version

God's Words of Life for Women of Color from
The African-American Devotional Bible,
King James Version.

God's Words of Life for Couples from the
New International Version

God's Words of Life for Students from the
New International Version

God's Words of Life for Teens from the
New International Version

More of God's Words of Life from the
Men's Devotional Bible, New International Version